Motivating Thoughts Of Bhagat Singh

Edited by

SHIKHA SHARMA

PRABHAT PRAKASHAN

Published by
PRABHAT PRAKASHAN PVT. LTD.
4/19 Asaf Ali Road,
New Delhi-110002 (INDIA)
e-mail: prabhatbooks@gmail.com

ISBN 978-93-5562-065-1
MOTIVATING THOUGHTS OF BHAGAT SINGH
Edited by Shikha Sharma

Edition
First, 2023

Price
₹ 300 (Rupees Three Hundred Only)

Printed at
Japan Art, Delhi

Editor's Note

In the annals of India's struggle for independence, few names shine as brightly as that of Shaheed Bhagat Singh. Born on the 28th of September 1907 in a Sandhu Jat family in Banga village of Jaranwala Tehsil, Punjab Province of British India (now in Pakistan's Punjab province), Bhagat Singh was destined to be a part of the fervent fight for liberty. Raised in a family deeply immersed in the pursuit of India's freedom, his father Sardar Kishan Singh and uncle Sardar Ajit Singh were esteemed freedom fighters of their time.

A beacon of inspiration and a founding member of the Hindustan Socialist Republican Association, Bhagat Singh played a pivotal role in shaping the course of the Indian Independence Movement. His indomitable spirit and the resounding catchphrase "Inquilab zindabad" (Long live the revolution) became emblematic of the struggle for a free India.

Tragically, Bhagat Singh embraced martyrdom at the age of 23. Alongside fellow freedom fighters Sukhdev Thapar and Shivaram Rajguru, he faced the gallows on 23rd March 1931 in Lahore jail, British India (now in Pakistan). Each year, India observes "Shaheed Diwas" on the same date, a solemn occasion to pay homage to the valiant sacrifice of Bhagat Singh, Sukhdev Thapar, and Shivaram Rajguru.

Shaheed Bhagat Singh remains an enduring symbol of unwavering courage and dedication to the cause of liberty. His words continue to resonate with the spirit of patriotism and determination in the hearts of millions.

In this book, we present a collection of Shaheed Bhagat Singh's powerful thoughts, translated into English. These inspiring thoughts serve as a testament to his vision and unwavering commitment to the nation's freedom struggle.

As we remember the life and sacrifice of this remarkable revolutionary, may these thoughts inspire us to cherish and protect the hard-earned independence of our great nation.

❑

Contents

❑

A Brief Biography of Bhagat Singh

India also known as Bharat, is a land of bravery and gallantry. In every part of India, brave people are found. This statement comes before us frequently and challengingly as we remember and discuss about the freedom struggle. When we think about the freedom struggle, we are filled with the grief at the fact that our beloved country, under the shackles of foreigners for centuries, was compelled to suffer at their hands but on the other hand, when we think of the sacrifice, bravery, courage, patriotism and love of the freedom fighters, then we are filled with pride.

In the inspirational line of freedom fighters, one honourable name is Sardar Bhagat Singh. He was born on September 27, 1907 in the village called Banga in the district of Lyallpur (now in Pakistan).

His father Sardar Kishan Singh and uncle Sardar Ajit Singh were great revolutionaries and patriots. At that time, two movements were active in the country. On one hand, foreign goods were boycotted and it was supported by moderate parties and on the other hand, there was the opposition of radical parties. Bhagat Singh's uncle, Sardar Ajit Singh was leading the radical group. Sardar Kishan Singh was a staunch supporter of that movement. At the time of his birth, his father and uncle were both in jail. But after sometime, both were released from the prison. Therefore, Bhagat Singh was regarded very fortunate for them.

Bhagat Singh was handsome like his father. In his childhood, everybody loved him. People were eager to hold him in their lap.

Sardar Kishan Singh was a farsighted and a serious man. He was expert in assessing the validity of time. Sardar Kishan Singh and Sardar Ajit Singh were involved in the revolutionary activities and the British Government came to know about this. The government was in search of an excuse through which Sardar Ajit Singh could be arrested. In fact, the British regime had planned to torture Ajit Singh and gradually kill him. But it was anticipated long ago by Sardar Kishan Singh, so he advised him to leave India and go to another country. In this way, the revolutionary uncle of Bhagat Singh left for abroad along with few revolutionary friends, leaving behind his young wife and other members of the family disheartened.

Once Bhagat Singh as a boy, went with his father to the farm. At that time he was only three years of age. A group of labourers were planting mango trees in his garden. Hardly had he reached the farm, the child Bhagat left his father and started running all around the field. Sometimes, he used to run, stumble and fall, rise up and immediately try to run again. Everybody present there, watched and enjoyed this playful activity of Bhagat Singh and laughed heartily. Suddenly, they saw the child Bhagat Singh had squatted on the floor, and seemed to be planting something.

Sardar Kishan Singh became curious and asked him "My dear son, what are you doing?"

The boy said, "Father, I am going to grow guns all over the field."

His father was overwhelmed with love and took him in his lap and kept caressing him for a long time.

Such was the personality of Bhagat Singh who had inherited revolutionary traits from his parents.

For elementary education, Bhagat Singh was admitted in the primary school of the village. He used to go to school with his friends in a happy mood. In school, the teachers and children used to love Bhagat Singh very much.

When he was in class IV, he used to ask his friends, "What will you become, when you grow up?" Few used to say, 'I will become a farmer', some said they would take up a job, few had ideas to run a shop or a business and others had plans to marry and establish families.

At this, child Bhagat Singh used to say, "Oh! Is this a thing to be done. Ask me what I want to be when I grow up."

When children used to ask, he used to say in a proud manner that "I will turn the Britishers out of the country."

Bhagat Singh was brilliant in his studies. There was plenty of revolutionary literature for him at home. While studying in the fourth class, he had finished almost all the books available at home.

The urge to revolt against the British had been in him for a long time. Bhagat Singh had a bitter experience of the fierce tortures by the British government on his family, when he was just 10-11 years old. On account of this, the seeds of hatred against the British regime were sown very early in his mind and increased gradually as time passed by.

Bhagat Singh studied at D.A.V. School, Navkot. As he reached Navkot, his spirit knew no bounds. He loved the free atmosphere of the village which greatly helped him in his studies.

In 1919, when Gandhiji entered Indian politics in an unprecedented manner, in the entire country a new wave spread. A boy of twelve years, Bhagat Singh was very much influenced by this wave. In his adolescent mind, the determination to fight and struggle against the British became more strengthened.

On 13 April, 1919, a meeting was organised peacefully in Jalianwala Bagh. Suddenly, General Dyer ordered his troops to open fire at the gathering. In this merciless massacre, hundreds of lives were lost and thousands of people were wounded.

When Bhagat Singh came to know about this cruel massacre, he was shocked. He became silent and started thinking deeply in seclusion.

Next day he started from his home for school at the predetermined time, but instead of reaching there, he directly reached Amritsar. At that time in Amritsar, there was heavy terror of police over there. Order was issued to fire at anyone found suspicious. But child Bhagat Singh, while facing challenges and dangers on the way stealthily somehow reached Jalianwala Bagh. After reaching there, he collected some soil from the park in his lunch box, put a little amount of sand coloured with the blood of martyrs and put a tilak of this on his forehead. After that he looked carefully everywhere and offered his salutations to martyrs with folded hands.

On the other hand, when Bhagat Singh did not reach his home at the scheduled time, his family members were worried. After sometime, when he came back, everybody heaved a sigh of relief. His family members became astonished after hearing where he had been.

The incident at Jalianwala Bagh massacre inflamed the youth of the nation. There was feeling of hatred towards the British everywhere.

On the call of Gandhiji, Bhagat Singh gave up his studies and engaged himself wholeheartedly in the service of the nation and the boycott of foreign goods. This was an important part of non-cooperation movement of Gandhiji but being angry at the violence of Chauri-Chaura incident, Gandhiji withdrew this movement in the midst. The time when Gandhiji made a call to Indians for non co-operation movement, people gave up their jobs and devoted themselves wholeheartedly to the cause of the nation. Students gave up their studies. Now when the movement was called off, people had to face a serious challenge, students were again compelled to take up their studies. Doors of government colleges and schools were closed in anticipation. A wave of anger and disenchantment spread amongst the younger generation.

Although, Gandhiji was deeply disheartened at the stopping of the movement in between, but in his view, the struggle for freedom was in fact a struggle for rights, and at the same time, a struggle for principles. He did not accept any form of deviation, he was a staunch supporter of non-violence. There was also a large group in the Congress who were divided over the opinion of Gandhiji. Lala Lajpat Rai was one of them. He had previously nurtured the determination for the freedom of the nation. He established a National College, where young revolutionaries were introduced to the tactics of revolution while being taught at the same time.

A thought was slowly nurturing in the mind of Bhagat Singh that the British could not be defeated by the weak policy of non-violence. So he turned a deaf ear to the non-violence policies of Gandhiji and tried to prepare himself wholeheartedly for a revolutionary movement. In the college library, there was a vast amount of revolutionary literature. Gradually, Bhagat Singh deeply engaged himself in the studies. Everybody in the college was influenced by his revolutionary thoughts. Bhagat Singh soon mixed with them.

He was himself engaged in the revolutionary activities day and night. Now his family members were troubled by the thought of marriage of Bhagat Singh. Soon a proposal came from a nice family which too was accepted. On the one hand, preparations were going on for his engagement but Bhagat Singh was in a bad condition. He had started the mission of service to the nation and he had nothing else to think of other than that. He wrote a letter to his father and silently left his home. His departure from the home shocked his parents. His grandmother fell severely ill, so Bhagat Singh had to return home. But he made his family promise him that in future no one would ask him for marriage. Now he engaged himself wholeheartedly to the cause of the nation. On July 29, 1927, while returning home, he had a loaded gun with him. He was careful and alert as usual. As soon as he landed on the platform of Amritsar, it seemed to him that perhaps someone was following him. Bhagat Singh somehow reached a house escaping the police dragnet. The owner of that house gave Bhagat Singh his full support. After the policemen left, Bhagat Singh left that house and reached the railway station and boarded the train to Lahore.

After reaching Lahore station, hardly had he walked a few steps when a gang of policeman surrounded him. He was arrested and taken to the police station.

After his arrest, Bhagat Singh was put inside the royal palace. For further investigation, Khan Bahadur Tasduk Hussain, who was investigating the Kakori Case came. There was a doubt in the police that perhaps Bhagat Singh was an accomplice in that incident. But Bhagat Singh refused to state his opinion when he was asked. Therefore, he was presented before the magistrate. There he proved himself innocent. The Magistrate ordered his release on bail. The bail amount was a considerable one. Even then Sardar Kishan Singh somehow arranged it for him. Bhagat Singh was freed of the charges and he returned home.

Sardar Kishan Singh knew that Bhagat Singh was a suspect of the government. Therefore, in order to divert the attention of the government he wanted to engage Bhagat Singh in some other work. He opened a dairy for Bhagat Singh and the total responsibility was now shouldered by him. It went well for some time, but somehow again

Bhagat Singh engaged himself completely in revolutionary activities.

He made an organization in association with a few revolutionaries which they named 'Hindustan Socialist Republican Army'. In the absence of Chandrashekhar Azad, Bhagat Singh was made the Commander-in-Chief of the organization.

In the year 1928, the Simon Commission visited India. This commission was opposed everywhere. At every place, protest marches were being organised. During one such protest march, there was a lathi-charge which seriously hurt Lala Lajpat Rai. He succumbed to the injuries after sometime.

All revolutionaries were infuriated by this incident. Bhagat Singh, Chandrashekhar Azad and other revolutionaries decided to avenge the death of Lala Lajpat Rai. Soon, he got a chance and killed police officer Saunders who was responsible for Lalaji's death, with the help of Chandrashekhar and Rajguru.

After that incident, the police were in hot pursuit of Bhagat Singh. He travelled to many places in disguise, learning about the revolutionary activities. He started planning for a big gang forcing the British government to take note of his demands. Just then it occurred to him, why not throw a bomb in the Central Assembly (Assembly hall); this idea was supported by other revolutionaries as well.

On 8th April, 1929 when the members were getting into the Assembly, Bhagat Singh and Batukeshwar Dutt also entered and sat in the visitors' gallery. As soon as the bill was passed by an ordinance of the viceroy, Bhagat Singh and Batukeshwar Dutt stood up and Bhagat Singh threw the bomb wrapped in newspaper into the treasury benches. The deafening blast created panic in the Assembly. In the meantime Bhagat Singh lobbed another bomb. Then with handbills denouncing the wrong policies of the British government, were thrown into the Assembly hall. The event had been planned with great care taking attention to detail the British policy, bumping into each other. Just then Bhagat Singh took out his loaded pistol and fired twice.

Bhagat Singh and Batukeshwar Dutt were arrested. When questioned, Bhagat refused to make any statement before the police. Whatever he had to say he said that he will say in the court.

On 12th June, 1929 Bhagat Singh and Batukeshwar Dutt were sentenced to life imprisonment. Bhagat Singh was sent to Mianwali Jail and Batukeshwar Dutt to Lahore jail. Bhagat Singh and other freedom fighters went on a hunger strike against bad conditions in the jail. The British Government got worried due to this strike. They tried many tricks to break the strike but the brave revolutionaries stuck to their resolve. To stay alive they drank only water. To break the strike, the jailor filled water pitchers with milk but nobody even touched them. They rather broke all the pitchers and the jailor replaced them with new one filled with milk which were again broken by the revolutionaries. There was great resentment in the whole country against that hunger strike. Ultimately the government had to concede and the 114 days long hunger strike ended.

On 5th May, 1930 Lahore conspiracy case started before a tribunal. Bhagat Singh and others were taken in a lorry to the new court set up at Punch House. In the first warning itself, the court echoed with the slogan of the revolutionary 'Inquilab Zindabad'.

The court proceedings started. Bhagat Singh began reciting the following lines—

Vatan ki abroo ka pas dekhen kaun karta hain.
Suna hai aaj maktal mein hamara imtihan hoga.
Elahi woh bhi din hoga, jab apna raj dekhenge,
Jab apni hi zameen hogi aur apna asman hoga.

On 5th Octobor, 1930 Bhagat Singh and other revolutionaries were treated to a feast in the jail. These brave freedom fighters understood the meaning of that last supper, but they were happy. After two days, a messenger of the tribunal read out the decision to the revolutionaries—Bhagat Singh, Rajguru and Sukhdev were awarded death sentence.

After this judgement, the family members started coming for the last meeting. When Bhagat Singh met his mother, he told her, "Mother you please do not come to take my dead body, because if you start weeping after seeing my dead body, then people will say Bhagat Singh's mother is crying."

The news of the death sentence was accepted by Bhagat Singh as a cherished gift. His resolve to become a martyr at the altar of motherland and give a new life to his motherland was fulfilled. On the day of the hanging, hundreds of people gathered outside the jail to see this epoch-making sight. Seeing this, the British Government preponed the execution. The gallows echoed with the slogans of Bhagat Singh, Sukhdev and Rajguru, both of whom stood on his left and right respectively.

Saying 'Inquilab Zindabad', the trio kissed that noose and happily tightened it round their necks. Just then the hangman pulled the noose and these great revolutionaries sacrificed their lives at the altar of Mother India. Thereafter the policeman took out the dead bodies to a place and hurriedly tried to cremate them. As this news spread, a massive crowd gathered and British policemen had to run for their lives leaving the half-burnt bodies. People respectfully claimed the dead bodies and completed the last rites with full honours. This unforgettable and supreme sacrifice brought a new awareness in the whole country.

'Shaheedon ki chitaon par lagenge her baras mele,
Vatan par marnewalon ka yahi baki nishan hoga.'

A hundred salutes to such brave sons of Mother India.

❑

Quotes of Bhagat Singh

- A college student cannot cling to any undue pride that may lead him to atheism.
- A God-believing Hindu might be expecting to be reborn as a king. A Muslim or a Christian might dream of the luxuries to enjoy in paradise and the reward he is to get for his sufferings and sacrifices.
- A hero's legacy lives on in the hearts of those who continue to be inspired by their noble deeds.
- A lasting legacy gets built on courage, determination, and selflessness.

- A leader inspires others to dream big, believe in themselves, and achieve their goals.
- A leader is someone who motivates and encourages others to strive for excellence.
- A leader is someone who stands up for the rights and welfare of the people.
- A leader serves his people with selflessness and dedication.
- A leader takes a stand for justice and fights against injustice.
- A leader takes responsibility for his actions, even in adversity.
- A leader works for the betterment of society and not just for personal gain.
- A legacy is about leaving a mark in the world that inspires future generations to strive for greatness.
- A legacy is built on courage, sacrifice, and unwavering principles.
- A legacy is created based on service to humanity and the greater good.

- A legacy is created based on service to humanity and the greater good.
- A legacy is not about leaving something behind but living a life worth remembering.
- A legacy is not about seeking recognition but about leaving a lasting impression on the hearts and minds of people.
- A legacy is the culmination of a life well-lived, dedicated to a noble cause.
- A man who claims to be a realist has to challenge the whole of the ancient faith.
- A man who claims to be a realist has to challenge the whole of the ancient faith. It crumbles down if it does not stand the onslaught of the reason.
- A martyr's courage and conviction inspire us to stand up for our rights, no matter the challenges.
- A martyr's courage and selflessness are a beacon of hope in dark times, showing us the path to righteousness.
- A martyr's legacy is a beacon of hope that lights the way for those who seek a better tomorrow.

- A martyr's legacy is etched in the hearts of those who continue to strive for a better world.

- A martyr's legacy transcends the boundaries of time, inspiring future generations to carry the torch of freedom.

- A martyr's sacrifice echoes through history, reminding us of the price paid for our cherished liberties.

- A martyr's sacrifice is a beacon of inspiration for generations to come, igniting the flames of revolution.

- A martyr's sacrifice is a clarion call to rise against injustice and oppression and to fight for what is right.

- A martyr's sacrifice symbolises his unwavering commitment to his principles of freedom and equality. A martyr's sacrifice can be physical, but their spirit and ideals forever inspire us to be unyielding.

- A martyr's sacrifice symbolises his unwavering commitment to his principles of freedom and equality. A martyr's sacrifice can be physical, but their spirit and ideals forever inspire us to be unyielding.

- A martyr's spirit lives on in the hearts of those who continue to fight for the rights of the oppressed.

- A martyr's spirit lives on in the hearts of those who continue to fight for the rights of the oppressed.
- A motivated heart beats with the rhythm of revolution, propelling us toward a brighter future.
- A motivated heart is a beacon of hope, inspiring others to join the fight for freedom.
- A motivated mind is a powerful force that can change the course of history.
- A motivated mind is a resilient force that can overcome every setback and keep moving forward.
- A motivated spirit is an unstoppable force that can shake the foundations of tyranny.
- A nation cannot be suppressed or overcome by crushing two insignificant units.
- A passionate heart beats with the rhythm of change, propelling us toward a brighter future.
- A passionate heart is a powerful force that can change the course of history.
- A passionate mind is a resilient force that can overcome every setback and pursue the dream.

- A passionate soul is a beacon of hope, inspiring others to join the fight for freedom.

- A passionate spirit is an unstoppable force that can shake the foundations of injustice.

- A patriot is not afraid to speak and stand up for what is right, even in adverse situations.

- A patriot is not someone who loves his country but who works actively to make it a better place.

- A patriot's love for his country is not blind but is rooted in a deep understanding of its strengths and weaknesses.

- A patriot's love for his country is not conditional but unwavering, even in the face of challenges and obstacles.

- A patriot's love for his country is not limited to borders but extends to all its people, regardless of caste, creed, or religion.

- A patriot's love for his country is not limited to words but manifests through actions and deeds.

- A revolutionary does not necessarily mean a man with bombs and revolvers.

- A revolutionary is the last person on earth to submit to bullying.
- A spirit of utter helplessness fills every stratum of our society, and terrorism is an effective means of restoring the proper spirits in society, without which progress will be difficult.
- A true fighter never gives up, as perseverance is the hallmark of a courageous and determined soul.
- A true leader inspires others with their vision and passion.
- A true leader instils hope and inspires others to believe in their capabilities.
- A true leader instils hope and inspires others to believe in their capabilities.
- A true leader is encouraged by a sense of purpose and a vision for a better future.
- A true leader is encouraged by a sense of purpose and a vision for a better future.
- A true leader leads by example and inspires others to follow.

- A true leader leads by example and inspires others to follow.

- A true leader leads with empathy, compassion, and fairness.

- A true leader leads with empathy, compassion, and fairness.

- A true legacy is a gift to future generations, a legacy that keeps on giving.

- A true legacy is a gift to future generations, a legacy that keeps on giving.

- A true legacy is created by standing up for what is right, even in adverse situations.

- A true legacy is created by standing up for what is right, even in adverse situations.

- A true legacy is eternal, as it steadily inspires long after one's physical presence is gone.

- A true legacy is eternal, as it steadily inspires long after one's physical presence is gone.

- A true patriot is guided by the principles like equality, freedom, and justice for all, without discrimination.

- A true patriot is guided by the principles like equality, freedom, and justice for all, without discrimination.
- An authentic patriot fights not just for his freedom but for the release of every citizen of his nation.

❑

- Be brave, and let your actions speak louder than your fears.
- Because our forefathers had set up their faith in some Supreme Being—the Almighty God—any man who dares to challenge the validity of that faith or the very existence of that Supreme Being shall have to be called an apostate, a renegade.
- Belief can soften hardships and even can make them pleasant. In God, man can find powerful consolation and support. Without Him, man has to depend upon himself. To stand upon one's legs amid storms and hurricanes is not a child's play. At such testing moments, vanity, if any, evaporates, and man cannot dare to defy the general beliefs because if he does, then

we must conclude that he has some other strengths than mere vanity.

- Belief in God is the outcome of mysticism, a natural consequence of depression.
- Believe in the power of change, for it can transform even the darkest of times into a brighter future.
- Bombs and pistols do not make a revolution. The sword of revolution gets sharpened on the whetting stone of ideas.
- Bravery is not a choice but a necessity for those who seek to make a difference.
- Bravery is not about the absence of weakness but the triumph over it.
- Bravery is not the absence of doubt but the determination to overcome it.
- Bravery is not the absence of fear but the courage to act despite it.
- Bravery is the antidote to oppression, the weapon of the oppressed.
- Bravery is the armour that protects the righteous and empowers them to fight for justice.

- Bravery is the fire that burns within, igniting the spirit of rebellion against oppression.
- Bravery is the fuel that propels revolution. It is the driving force for change.
- Bravery is the legacy of those who fought for freedom, and we must carry it forward.
- Bravery is the mark of a true leader who fearlessly leads by example.
- Bravery is the willingness to sacrifice for the greater good without seeking personal gain.
- Bravery is unwavering faith in the righteousness of one's cause, regardless of the challenges.
- Bravery never gets restricted by age, gender, or background because it is the spirit of the indomitable human soul.
- Britishers hurled an inhuman and barbarous measure on the devoted heads of the representatives of India, and the starving and struggling millions got deprived of their primary right; the sole means of improving their economic welfare.
- By revolution, we mean that the present order of things, which manifests injustice, must change.

- By revolution, we mean the end of the miseries of capitalist wars. It is only proper to pronounce judgment with an understanding of our aims and objectives and the process of achieving them.

- By revolution, we mean the ultimate establishment of an order of society that is not intimidated by such breakdown, in which the sovereignty of the proletariat gets recognised, and a world federation should redeem humanity from the bondage of capitalism and the misery of imperial wars.

❑

- Certain people in the labour movement enlist some absurd ideas about the economic liberty of the peasants and workers without political freedom. They are demagogues or muddle-headed people.
- Change begins with a single step taken by a courageous individual who dares to challenge the status quo.
- Change is not a choice but a necessity for society's progress and humanity's betterment.
- Change is not a destination but a journey that requires continuous effort and unwavering commitment.
- Change is not a one-time event but a continuous process that requires constant vigilance and unwavering commitment.

- Change is not easy, but it is necessary for growth and worth fighting for.
- Change is not for the faint of heart but for those willing to stand up and fight for what is right.
- Change is the birthright of every individual, and we must claim it and make it a reality.
- Change is the force that breaks the shackles of conformity and empowers individuals to rise above mediocrity.
- Change is the inevitable force that drives progress and propels society forward.
- Change is the legacy of those who dared to challenge the status quo and fought for justice.
- Change is the light that dispels the darkness of oppression and paves the way for a brighter future.
- Change is the product of collective effort, and it requires the unity and determination of the masses.
- Change is the revolution that sparks the flame of hope and fuels the fire of transformation.
- Change is the wind of transformation that blows away the dust of oppression and ushers in a new era of freedom.

- Change manifests our dreams and aspirations, and our responsibility is to make it a reality.
- Change may come slowly, but it results from unwavering perseverance and belief.
- Change may face resistance, but it is the force that breaks through barriers and paves the way for progress.
- Change results from a collective conscience, the development of the masses rising for a common cause.
- Circumstances may tilt the scales of justice, but our determination to seek justice should never waver.
- Courage is not a fleeting emotion but a steadfast commitment to standing up for what is right, regardless of the obstacles.
- Courage is not the absence of fear but the triumph over it. Have the courage to stand up for what you believe in.
- Courage is the armour that protects our convictions and empowers us to challenge injustice.
- Courage is the bridge that connects our dreams to reality, and we must cross it with unwavering determination.

- Courage is the driving force that empowers us to break free from the shackles of oppression and fight for our freedom.
- Courage is the foundation of all virtues, and bravery is the embodiment of courage.
- Courage is the foundation of revolution, resistance, and the cornerstone of change.
- Courage is the fuel that drives us to take risks, challenge the status quo, and create a better world for future generations.
- Courage is the fuel that ignites the fire of revolution and propels us to fight for our rights.
- Courage is the guiding star that leads us on the path of righteousness, even when the way seems uncertain.
- Courage is the hallmark of a genuine revolutionary who dares to dream and fight for it.
- Courage is the hallmark of a true leader, who leads by example and inspires others to follow their convictions.
- Courage is the inner strength that encourages us to stand up for truth, justice, and freedom, no matter the consequences.

- Courage is the key that unlocks the door to bravery, and fear is just a hurdle to overcome.
- Courage is the legacy of those who stood up against tyranny, refused to bow to oppression, and fought for justice until their last breath.
- Courage is the light that guides us through the darkest of times and leads us to the path of righteousness.
- Courage is the power that empowers us to break through the chains of oppression and strive for a brighter future.
- Courage is the soul of resistance, the essence of defiance, and the heart of rebellion.
- Courage is the spark that ignites the flame of revolution and inspires others to join the fight for freedom.
- Courage is the strength that enables us to confront challenges head-on, stand tall in the face of adversity, and never give up on our dreams.
- Courage is the unwavering belief in our cause, the steadfast commitment to our ideals, and the relentless determination to make a difference.

- Courage is the unwavering resolve to speak up for the voiceless, fight for the oppressed, and to seek equality for all.
- Courage is the virtue that enables us to persevere in the face of adversity and never back from our principles.
- Courage is the weapon of the brave, the shield of the righteous, and the antidote to fear.
- Courage is the willingness to face adversity and take action, even in the face of overwhelming odds.
- Crime is the most severe social problem which needs very discreet treatment.
- Criticism and independent thinking are the two indispensable qualities of a revolutionary
- Crush your individuality first. Shake off the dreams of personal comfort. Then start to work. Inch by inch, you shall have to proceed. It needs courage, perseverance, and unyielding determination. No difficulties and no hardships shall discourage you. No failure and betrayal shall dishearten you. No travails imposed upon you shall snuff out the revolutionary

will in you. Through the ordeal of suffering and sacrifice, you shall come out victorious. And these individual victories shall be the valuable assets of the revolution.

❑

- Death should not be a means to escape worldly difficulties.
- Defiance is standing tall when others want us to kneel and uphold our principles despite the odds.
- Defiance is standing up against oppression, even when it seems impossible, because it is better to die with honour than to live in chains.
- Defiance is standing up for what is right, even when it is unpopular because our moral obligation is to resist oppression and fight for justice.
- Defiance is the cornerstone of change, the rock upon which revolutions build, and the driving force of social transformation.

- Defiance is the courage to resist, the audacity to rebel, and the determination to create a better world.
- Defiance is the fire that burns within us, the passion that fuels our fight for freedom, and the unwavering resolve to never back down.
- Defiance is the fuel that ignites the fire of revolution and inspires us to challenge the status quo.
- Defiance is the legacy of those who stood against tyranny, challenged oppressive systems, and paved the way for a better future.
- Defiance is the light that guides us through the darkness of oppression, the compass that directs us toward the path of freedom, and the driving force that propels us forward.
- Defiance is the mark of a genuine revolutionary who dares to question authority, refuses to be silenced, and fights for the rights of the oppressed.
- Defiance is the power that empowers us to break free from the chains of conformity and fight for our rights.
- Defiance is the refusal to accept limitations imposed by others, the determination to break through barriers, and the unwavering belief in our potential.

- Defiance is the refusal to accept the unacceptable, the determination to challenge the unjust, and the resolve to resist tyranny.
- Defiance is the refusal to bow to injustice, the unwavering stand against oppression, and the unyielding spirit of resistance.
- Defiance is the refusal to conform to societal norms perpetuating injustice and inequality and the resolve to break free from oppression.
- Defiance is the spark that ignites the flame of revolution, the driving force that propels us to challenge unjust systems, and the legacy of those who refused to bow down.
- Defiance is the spirit that refuses to be silent, the voice that speaks up for the voiceless, and the unwavering stand against injustice.
- Defiance is the unwavering commitment to our beliefs, the refusal to compromise our values, and the courage to stand up for what is right.
- Defiance is the voice of the oppressed, the language of the marginalized, and the cry for freedom.

- Defiance is the weapon of the brave, the shield of the oppressed, and the beacon of hope for those who seek justice.
- Despite all the denunciations and condemnation of their friends and kins and ruthless repression and persecution of the foreign government, a party of young men will ever live to teach a lesson to the arrogant rulers.
- Despite being the most necessary element of society, producers or labourers, are robbed by their exploiters of their labour and deprived of their elementary rights.
- Destruction is not only essential but indispensable for construction.
- Determination is the backbone of success, achievement, and unwavering belief in our potential.
- Determination is the belief in our potential, the unwavering faith in our abilities, and the persistent effort to reach our goals.
- Determination is the courage to go against the tide, challenge the status quo, and stand up for what we believe in.

- Determination is the courage to take risks, the resolve to face challenges head-on, and the commitment to never back down.
- Determination is the driving force that propels us forward, the inner fire that keeps us going, and the unshakable faith in our abilities.
- Determination is the driving force that propels us toward our vision, the unwavering commitment to our cause, and the resilience to keep pushing forward.
- Determination is the fire that burns within us, the passion that fuels our actions, and the unwavering faith in our abilities.
- Determination is the firm resolve to make a difference, the unwavering stand for what is just, and the persistent effort toward positive change.
- Determination is the fuel that keeps us going, even when the odds get stacked against us, and the challenges seem insurmountable.
- Determination is the grit that propels us forward, even in the face of adversity and the unwavering belief in our capabilities.

- Determination is the key that unlocks the door to success, the bridge that connects our dreams to reality, and the driving force behind every achievement.
- Determination is the mindset that turns challenges into opportunities, setbacks into lessons, and failures into stepping stones toward success.
- Determination is the refusal to settle for mediocrity, the hunger for excellence, and the relentless pursuit of our aspirations.
- Determination is the resilience that keeps us going, even when the going gets tough, and the motivation to never give up on our dreams.
- Determination is the spirit that refuses to be deterred by failures, setbacks, or obstacles and keeps striving toward the desired outcome.
- Determination is the strength that arises from within, the indomitable spirit that rises above all hurdles, and the tenacity to keep moving forward.
- Determination is the strength that empowers us to overcome obstacles, persevere through hardships, and never give up on our dreams.

- Determination is the unwavering commitment to our ideals, the perseverance to overcome obstacles, and the unshakable belief in our purpose.
- Determination is the unwavering pursuit of truth, the relentless fight against injustice, and the steadfast commitment to our principles.
- Determination is the unwavering resolve to achieve our goals, no matter how difficult the path may be.
- Determination is the unwavering stand for what is right, the unyielding fight for justice, and the relentless pursuit of freedom.
- Devotion embodies love, sacrifice, and service, the unwavering commitment to the welfare of all, and the selfless pursuit of a better tomorrow.
- Devotion embodies sacrifice, the willingness to put others before oneself, and the unwavering dedication to a noble cause.
- Devotion is sacrificing personal interests for the greater good, the unwavering commitment to a higher cause, and selfless service to humanity.
- Devotion is surrendering one's interests for the more significant benefit of humanity, the selfless act of giving without expecting anything in return.

- Devotion is the act of giving without expecting anything in return, selfless service to humanity, and the unwavering commitment to making a difference.
- Devotion is the backbone of social change, the unwavering determination to fight against injustice, and selfless service to the marginalized.
- Devotion is the commitment to a vision, the unwavering loyalty to a principle, and the relentless pursuit of justice.
- Devotion is the courage to fight for what is right, the unwavering determination to bring about positive change, and the selfless service to the cause of freedom.
- Devotion is the courage to stand up for what is right, the unwavering stand for truth, and the selfless service to the nation.
- Devotion is the fire that burns within, the passion that drives us to serve a cause with all our hearts and soul.
- Devotion is the fuel that drives us toward our goals, the unwavering belief in our cause, and the relentless pursuit of our dreams.

- Devotion is the highest form of love for one's country, selfless dedication to the welfare of the people, and unwavering loyalty to the nation.
- Devotion is the moral compass that guides our actions, the unwavering adherence to our values, and the selfless service to humanity.
- Devotion is the passion that propels us forward, the unwavering commitment to our principles, and the relentless pursuit of our vision.
- Devotion is the relentless pursuit of one's beliefs, the unwavering faith in a higher purpose, and the sacrifice for the greater good.
- Devotion is the spirit of selflessness, the unwavering dedication to the welfare of others, and the relentless pursuit of a just society.
- Devotion is the unshakable faith in one's ideals, the relentless determination to bring about positive change, and tireless efforts toward the greater good.
- Devotion is the unwavering belief in the power of truth, the selfless commitment to justice, and the tireless efforts toward social upliftment.

- Devotion is the unwavering commitment to a cause larger than oneself, the selfless dedication to the betterment of society.
- Do not fear change, for it is the precursor to progress and the catalyst for revolution.
- Do not lose patience and sense at one time and hope at another. Try to make stability and determination second nature to yourselves.
- Don't ask for rights; take them. And don't let anyone give them to you. Rights handed to you for nothing have something that matters with it. It's more than likely it is only a wrong turned inside out.
- Don't interpret the word 'revolution' in a literal sense. Various meanings and significances are attributed to this word, according to the interests of those who use or misuse it.

❑

E

- Education is the only weapon to be employed.
- Embrace change, the only constant in life, and adapt to it with courage and determination.
- Embrace the power of intellect, for it is the fuel that ignites the flames of change.
- Embrace the power of intellectualism, for it is the key to unlocking your true potential.
- Empathy is the ability to understand and share the feelings of others, the cornerstone of compassion and humanity.
- Empathy is the antidote to indifference, the understanding of the suffering of others, and the resolve to take action for their well-being.

- Empathy is the bridge that connects hearts, the understanding of the plight of the oppressed, and the resolve to fight for their rights.

- Empathy is the catalyst for positive change, the understanding of the systemic injustices faced by the marginalized, and the determination to challenge and overcome them.

- Empathy is the cornerstone of social justice, the ability to stand in solidarity with the marginalized, and the unwavering commitment to their upliftment.

- Empathy is the driving force behind altruism, the selfless act of putting oneself in the shoes of others and taking action for their welfare.

- Empathy is the driving force behind social progress, the understanding of the injustices faced by the marginalized, and the determination to bring about positive change.

- Empathy is the essence of authentic leadership, the ability to connect with the emotions of others and the commitment to serve the common good.

- Empathy is the essence of humanity, the capacity to feel the joy and pain of others and the unwavering commitment to creating a more compassionate world.

- Empathy is the flame that ignites the fire of social change, the understanding of the struggles of others, and the determination to fight for their rights.
- Empathy is the foundation of a just society, the ability to understand the perspectives of others and the commitment to creating a world where everyone gets treated with dignity and respect.
- Empathy is the foundation of equality, the ability to understand and acknowledge the diversity of human experiences, and the commitment to creating a world where everyone gets treated equally.
- Empathy is the hallmark of a just society, the ability to understand and empathize with the experiences of others, and the commitment to create a better society for all.
- Empathy is the heart of social activism, the ability to understand the struggles of others and the unwavering commitment to fight for their dignity and rights.
- Empathy is the heart of social change, the capacity to feel the pain and suffering of others and the motivation to alleviate it.

- Empathy is the key that unlocks the door to compassion, the understanding of the struggles of others, and the resolve to make a difference.
- Empathy is the light that guides us toward social transformation, the ability to connect with the emotions of others and the unwavering commitment to social justice.
- Empathy is the moral compass that guides our actions, the ability to see the world through the eyes of others, and the commitment to fight for our rights.
- Empathy is the power that unites us, the understanding of the common human experience, and the resolve to fight against discrimination and oppression.
- Empathy is the soul of humanity, the capacity to feel the pain and suffering of others as our own, and the determination to bring about positive change.
- Empower yourself with the power of intellect, and nothing can hold you back.
- Empowerment is the antidote to inequality, the belief that everyone has the right to get respected with dignity.

- Empowerment is the birthright of every individual, the belief that we have the inherent strength to overcome any obstacle.
- Empowerment is the bridge that connects individuals to their inner strength, the understanding that we have the power to overcome challenges and obstacles.
- Empowerment is the catalyst for social revolution, the understanding that when individuals are empowered, they can change the course of history.
- Empowerment is the cornerstone of freedom, the understanding that true freedom comes from within and cannot be granted or taken away by others.
- Empowerment is the driving force behind the social transformation, the understanding that when individuals are empowered, they can create a better social environment.
- Empowerment is the essence of authentic leadership, the belief that leaders should empower others to achieve their fullest potential.
- Empowerment is the essence of true democracy, the belief that everyone has the right to participate and contribute to the decision-making process.

- Empowerment is the flame that ignites the fire of change, the belief that we have the power to transform ourselves and our communities.
- Empowerment is the force that propels us toward our goals, the belief that we can achieve greatness.
- Empowerment is the foundation of social justice, the understanding that when individuals are empowered, they can fight against oppression and injustice.
- Empowerment is the foundation of social progress, the understanding that societies can transform and evolve when individuals are empowered.
- Empowerment is the fuel that drives the engine of social change, the belief that every individual has the power to make a difference.
- Empowerment is the fuel that energizes us to fight against injustice, the realisation that we have the power to stand up for our rights.
- Empowerment is the key that unlocks the potential within, the realisation that we have the power to shape our destiny.
- Empowerment is the key to breaking free from the shackles of oppression, the realisation that we have

the power to challenge and overcome any form of discrimination.

- Empowerment is the key to unlocking human potential, the realisation that we have the power to achieve our dreams and aspirations.
- Empowerment is the light that dispels the darkness of ignorance and oppression, the belief that knowledge is power.
- Empowerment is the path to self-determination, the realisation that we have the right to control our lives and destinies.
- Empowerment is the path to self-liberation, the belief that we have the power to break free from the chains of oppression.
- Empowerment is the spirit that drives us forward, the understanding that we can shape our destinies and create a better future.
- Empowerment is the weapon of the oppressed, the realisation that no one can take away our power without our consent.
- Equality is the antidote to discrimination, the realisation that no one should be judged or treated differently based on their caste, creed, or religion.

- Equality is the beacon of hope, the understanding that we are all equal in justice's eyes and get treated as such.
- Equality is the bridge that connects us all, the understanding that we are all equal citizens of the same nation and should have equal rights and opportunities.
- Equality is the cornerstone of a just society, the belief that everyone deserves to be treated fairly and with dignity.
- Equality is the driving force behind social change, the understanding that societies can transform and evolve when all individuals get treated equally.
- Equality is the essence of humanity, the belief that all human beings are equal regardless of their social status or background.
- Equality is the essence of humanity, the understanding that all human beings are equal and should be treated as such, regardless of their differences.
- Equality is the essence of true democracy, the belief that every individual should have equal rights and opportunities to participate in democratic process.

- Equality is the essence of unity, the belief that we are all equal members of the same human family and should treat each other with love and respect.
- Equality is the force that breaks barriers, the belief that everyone should have equal access to opportunities and resources.
- Equality is the foundation of a harmonious society, the realisation that no one should be marginalized or discriminated against based on their identity.
- Equality is the foundation of a just society, the belief that no one should be oppressed or discriminated against based on caste, gender, or religion.
- Equality is the foundation of freedom, the understanding that all individuals are born equal and should have equal opportunities in life.
- Equality is the fuel that drives social change, the understanding that all individuals should have equal opportunities to succeed and thrive.
- Equality is the light that shines on the path of social justice, the realisation that no one should be denied their fundamental rights and freedoms.

- Equality is the path to true liberation, the belief that everyone should have equal rights and opportunities to live a life of dignity and freedom.
- Equality is the pillar of social justice, the realisation that everyone should have equal access to resources, opportunities, and rights.
- Equality is the pillar of social progress, the realisation that when all individuals get treated equally, societies can thrive and prosper.
- Equality is the soul of democracy, the understanding that everyone should have equal rights and opportunities to participate in decision-making.
- Equality is the vision of a better world, the belief that everyone deserves to be treated with respect, regardless of gender, race, or religion.
- Equality is the voice of the oppressed, the understanding that everyone deserves to have their rights and dignity respected, regardless of their social standing.
- Equality is the weapon of the oppressed, the belief that everyone should have equal access to resources and opportunities, regardless of their background.

- Every tiny molecule of ash is in motion with my heat. I am such a lunatic that I am free even in jail.
- Everybody can become great if he strives.

❑

- Fear may knock at your door, but bravery is what keeps it from entering.
- Fearlessness embodies courage, the refusal to be silenced or intimidated in the face of oppression.
- Fearlessness embodies resilience, the determination to never give up while facing challenges.
- Fearlessness embodies self-belief, the confidence to pursue your dreams without fear of failure.
- Fearlessness is not the absence of fear but the triumph over it.
- Fearlessness is the armour that protects your convictions and principles from being swayed by fear.

- Fearlessness is the attitude of persistence, the determination to pursue justice and equality without fear of consequences.
- Fearlessness is the attitude of the invincible, refusing to return in the face of adversity.
- Fearlessness is the beacon of hope in times of darkness, the unwavering faith in the power of righteousness.
- Fearlessness is the driving force behind revolutions, the audacity to challenge oppressive systems.
- Fearlessness is the driving force of change, the determination to challenge the status quo and create a better world.
- Fearlessness is the driving force of progress, the willingness to take risks and push boundaries.
- Fearlessness is the embodiment of bravery, the courage to confront your fears and overcome them.
- Fearlessness is the essence of bravery, the courage to confront one's fears and overcome them.
- Fearlessness is the essence of liberation, the belief that nothing can hold one back from pursuing their dreams and ideals.

- Fearlessness is the essence of rebellion, the refusal to bow to unjust authority.
- Fearlessness is the essence of revolution, the readiness to face any obstacle or danger in pursuing freedom.
- Fearlessness is the fire that burns within, driving one to fight for the rights of the oppressed and marginalized.
- Fearlessness is the foundation of change, the conviction to stand up for what is right, no matter how difficult the path may be.
- Fearlessness is the foundation of courage, the readiness to face any obstacle in pursuit of your ideals.
- Fearlessness is the fuel that propels you toward your goals, regardless of obstacles or setbacks.
- Fearlessness is the guiding light in the darkness of injustice, the unwavering faith in the power of righteousness.
- Fearlessness is the guiding light that leads you toward your purpose, even amid uncertainty.

- Fearlessness is the hallmark of a true patriot, the willingness to sacrifice everything for the nation's cause.
- Fearlessness is the hallmark of a true revolutionary, the refusal to cower in the face of adversity.
- Fearlessness is the key to unlocking your true potential and achieving greatness.
- Fearlessness is the legacy of the brave, the inspiration to never back in the face of fear.
- Fearlessness is the legacy of the brave, the inspiration to stand up and fight for what is just.
- Fearlessness is the mark of a true hero, the courage to face the unknown and fight for what is just.
- Fearlessness is the mark of a true leader, the ability to inspire and motivate others despite facing fear.
- Fearlessness is the mark of authentic leadership, the ability to face challenges and adversity without succumbing to fear.
- Fearlessness is the mindset that allows you to break free from the chains of fear and take bold actions.
- Fearlessness is the path to freedom, the courage to rise above fear and fight for what is right.

- Fearlessness is the path to true freedom, the courage to break free from fear and oppression.
- Fearlessness is the soul of resistance, the strength to stand up against oppression and fight for the rights of the oppressed.
- Fearlessness is the spirit of defiance, the refusal to succumb to fear and intimidation.
- Fearlessness is the spirit of defiance, the unwavering determination to challenge the world's injustices.
- Fearlessness is the spirit of martyrdom, the readiness to sacrifice everything for the greater good.
- Fearlessness is the spirit of rebellion, the defiance against oppressive systems, and the courage to break free.
- Fearlessness is the spirit of resilience and unwavering determination never to surrender when facing challenges.
- Fearlessness is the spirit of revolution, the audacity to challenge the norm and pave the way for change.
- Fearlessness is the spirit of revolution, the daring to challenge the status quo and fight for freedom.

- Fearlessness is the spirit that empowers you to rise above limitations and reach for the stars.
- Fearlessness is the strength of the oppressed, the refusal to bow to tyranny and injustice.
- Fearlessness is the strength of the righteous, the unshakable belief in the power of truth and justice.
- Fearlessness is the strength that encourages you to challenge the norms and question the status quo.
- Fearlessness is the unwavering belief in your principles and the courage to defend them, no matter the consequences.
- Fearlessness is the unwavering spirit that leads to victory, the strength to overcome all obstacles and achieve greatness.
- Fearlessness is the virtue that empowers you to stand up for what is right, even in the face of adversity.
- Fearlessness is the weapon of the brave, the unwavering courage to stand up for what is right.
- Fight for your beliefs, and let your activism speak louder than your words.
- For mass struggles, nonviolence is essential.

- For selfish motives, I am not going to pray.
- For us, compromise never means surrender but a step forward and some rest. That is all and nothing else. For us, compromise never means submission but a step forward and some rest.
- Force, when aggressively applied, is violence and is morally unjustifiable. Still, when used to further a legitimate cause, it has its moral justification—eliminating force at all costs in Utopian.
- Freedom embodies courage, the willingness to fight for what is just and proper.
- Freedom embodies dignity, the right to live with self-respect and honour.
- Freedom is not a privilege but a birthright of every individual.
- Freedom is not just a concept but a living reality that should be cherished and safeguarded at all costs.
- Freedom is not just a concept but a state of being that empowers individuals to reach their fullest potential.
- Freedom is not just a privilege but a fundamental human right that should be cherished and protected.

- Freedom is the air that fills the lungs of a nation, and it is the birthright of every citizen.
- Freedom is the beacon of hope in times of darkness, the light that guides us toward a better future.
- Freedom is the birthright of every individual, regardless of caste, creed, or religion.
- Freedom is the cornerstone of a just and equitable society and is a cause worth dedicating one's life to.
- Freedom is the essence of humanity, the driving force behind progress and growth.
- Freedom is the flame of resistance that burns in the hearts of those who strive for change.
- Freedom is the foundation of democracy, the pillar of a just society.
- Freedom is the foundation of justice, a just and equitable society.
- Freedom is the fuel that ignites the fire of courage, empowering us to stand up for our rights.
- Freedom is the heartbeat of democracy, the pulse that keeps our nation alive.

- Freedom is the highest form of expression, the right to voice our opinions and beliefs.
- Freedom is the imperishable birthright of all.
- Freedom is the legacy of those who fought for it, the duty of those who cherish it.
- Freedom is the lifeline of a nation, the breath that sustains its people.
- Freedom is the light that shines in the darkness of oppression, guiding us toward a better tomorrow.
- Freedom is the melody of revolution, the anthem of those who dare to challenge injustice.
- Freedom is the oxygen of democracy, and it is the responsibility of every citizen to protect and uphold it.
- Freedom is the oxygen of the soul, the essence of human existence.
- Freedom is the path to progress, leading to a brighter and better future.
- Freedom is the precious gift that our forefathers fought for, and it's our responsibility to preserve and protect it.

- Freedom is the soul's desire to soar high and reach for the skies, unshackled by limitations.
- Freedom is the soul's expression of its inherent rights, the essence of being human.
- Freedom is the soul's longing for independence, the yearning to break free from chains of oppression.
- Freedom is the spirit of revolution, the power to shake the foundations of tyranny.
- Freedom is the ultimate prize worth striving for, the goal that defines the human spirit.
- Freedom is the voice of dissent, the right to question and challenge authority.
- Freedom is the voice of the oppressed, the hope of the downtrodden, and the right of every individual.

❑

- God came into imaginary existence to encourage man to face all the trying circumstances boldly, to meet all dangers manfully, and to check and restrain his outbursts in prosperity and affluence.
- God, both with his private laws and parental generosity, was imagined and painted in greater detail.
- Grow! Every minute of your life, you must think of devising means of that this ancient land may arise with flaming eyes and fierce yawns.

❑

- Here in India, as in other countries in the past, terrorism will develop into a revolution and the revolution into independence, social, political, and economic.
- I am a man and nothing more. None can claim to be more. I also have this weakness in me.
- I am a man, and all that affects humankind concerns me.
- I am neither a poet nor a litterateur nor a journalist nor a critic.
- I am neither a rival nor an incarnation nor the Supreme Being Myself.
- I ask why your Omnipotent God does not hold a man back when he is about to commit a sin or offence. It is

child's play for God. Why did He not kill warlords? Why did He not remove the fury of war from their minds? This way, God could have saved humanity from great calamity and horror.

- I deny the very existence of that Almighty Supreme Being.

- I emphasize that I am full of ambition, hope, and life's natural charm. But I can renounce all at the time of need, and that is the real sacrifice.

- I know in the present circumstances, my faith in God would have made my life easier, my burden lighter, and my disbelief in Him has turned all the events too dry, and the situation may assume too rough a shape. A bit of mysticism makes it poetic. But I do not want the help of any intoxication to meet my fate. I am a realist. I have been trying to overpower the instinct in me with the help of reason. I have only sometimes been successful in achieving this end. But man must try and endeavour; success depends upon chance and environment.

- I was a confirmed atheist then, and I am an atheist now. It was not an easy task to face that ordeal. Beliefs make it easier to go through hardships, even make them pleasant. Man can find strong support in God and an encouraging consolation in His Name. If you have no belief in Him, then there is no alternative but to depend upon yourself. Standing firm on your feet amid storms and strong winds is not child's play. In difficult times, vanity, if it remains, evaporates, and man cannot find the courage to defy beliefs held in common esteem by the people. If he revolts against such ideas, we must conclude that it is not sheer vanity; he has some extraordinary strength.

- If a man becomes a revolutionary and goes about with his life in the hollow of his hand, ready to sacrifice it at any moment, he does not do so merely for the fun of it.

- If the deaf is to hear, the sound has to be very loud. When we dropped the bomb, we did not intend to kill anybody. We have bombed the British Government. The British must quit India and make her independent.

- If we ignore the motive, the most prominent general of the world will appear like an ordinary murderer; revenue officers will look like thieves and cheaters.

- If we set aside the motive, then Jesus Christ will appear to be a man responsible for creating disturbances, breaking the peace, and preaching revolt and will be considered to be a dangerous personality in the language of the law. But we worship him.

- If you are a businessman, an established worldly, or a family man, please don't play with fire.

- If, after considerable reasoning, one believes in any theory or philosophy, his faith is welcomed.

- If, as you believe, there is an Almighty, Omnipresent, Omniscient God, who created the earth or universe, please let me know, first of all, why he created this world. This world is full of woe, grief, and countless miseries, where not even one person lives in peace. Where is God? What is He doing? Is He getting a diseased pleasure out of it? A Nero! A Genghis Khan! Down with Him!

- Ignore the motive; every religious preacher will get dubbed as a preacher of falsehoods, every religious preacher will get anointed as a preacher of lies, and every prophet will get charged with misguiding crores of simple and ignorant people.

- In adversity, perseverance becomes our most potent weapon to overcome any obstacle.

- In adversity, revolution is the unwavering resolve to fight for what is right, no matter the challenges.
- In adversity, revolutionaries remain resolute, never backing from their principles and ideals.
- In adversity, revolutionaries stand tall and unyielding in pursuing a just and equitable society.
- In India alone, Buddhism and Jainism are sometimes entirely separate from Brahmanism, in which there are again some conflicting faiths such as Arya Samaj and Sanatan Dharma.
- In pursuing freedom, resilience is the unwavering faith in the cause and the determination to overcome all obstacles.
- In pursuing freedom, resistance is the unwavering commitment to the cause, despite all the obstacles.
- In pursuing freedom, revolution is the unwavering commitment to the cause and the determination to bring about change.
- In pursuing justice and equality, sacrifice becomes a noble duty that revolutionaries willingly embrace.
- In pursuing justice and freedom, selflessness becomes a guiding principle that revolutionaries embrace with open hearts.

- In pursuing justice, resistance is the unwavering determination to challenge the status quo and demand change.
- In pursuing justice, resistance is the unwavering stand for truth and the refusal to compromise.
- In pursuing justice, revolution is the unwavering commitment to the cause and the resilience to face all obstacles.
- In the darkest of times, let your dreams shine bright with inspiration.
- In the face of adversity, bravery shines the brightest, illuminating the way to victory.
- In the face of adversity, resilience is the key that unlocks the door to success, empowering us to rise above our circumstances.
- In the face of adversity, resilience is the light that guides us forward, even in darkness.
- In the face of adversity, resilience is the unwavering belief in our abilities and the refusal to back down.
- In the face of adversity, resistance is the bold and fearless act of defiance, standing firm in the face of oppression.

- In the face of adversity, resistance is the indomitable spirit that keeps us going, even when the odds are against us.
- In the face of challenges, let inspiration be your strength.
- In the face of challenges, perseverance is our shield that protects our dreams from being shattered.
- In the face of challenges, perseverance is the virtue that separates the ordinary from the extraordinary.
- In the face of hardships, resilience is the unwavering determination to keep moving forward, never giving up on our dreams.
- In the face of injustice, bravery is the beacon of hope that lights the way to freedom.
- In the face of injustice, revolution is the courage to stand up and speak out, no matter the consequences.
- In the face of oppression, rebellion is the tool that empowers the powerless, giving voice to the voiceless.
- In the fight against injustice, revolutionaries are the trailblazers who blaze a path for others to follow.

- In the future society, i.e., the Communist society we want to build, we will not establish charitable institutions. Still, there shall be no needy and poor and no almsgiving and alms taking.
- In the future society, when people adjust the relations of various elements based on equality, the producers and the distributors shall be considered equally important.
- In the journey toward freedom, resilience is the unwavering commitment to the cause, despite all the obstacles.
- In the name of those gallant men and women who willingly accepted death so that we, their descendants, may lead a happier life, who toiled ceaselessly and perished for the poor, the hungry, and exploited millions of India, we call upon every patriot to take up the fight in all seriousness.
- In the political field, the liberals wanted some reform under the present government. At the same time, the extremists demanded a bit more and were prepared to employ radical means for the same purpose.
- In the pursuit of freedom, inspiration is our guiding light.

- In the pursuit of justice, no sacrifice is too great.
- Indians shall play their destined role when all calculations prove futile. The wise and the mighty shall be bewildered by the simple and the weak when great empires crumble. New nations shall arise and surprise humanity with the splendour and glory which shall be all it is own.
- Injustice anywhere is a threat to justice everywhere, and activism is the answer.
- Inspiration is the catalyst for transformation, propelling us toward our destiny.
- Inspiration is the compass that points us toward our true purpose.
- Inspiration is the driving force that propels us toward our goals.
- Inspiration is the fuel that empowers us to overcome all obstacles.
- Inspiration is the key that unlocks the door to greatness.
- Inspiration is the light that dispels the darkness of doubt.

- Inspiration is the seed from which greatness grows.
- Inspiration is the spark that ignites the flames of change.
- Inspirational dreams are the foundation of a brighter tomorrow.
- Intellectualism is the ally of freedom, equipping us with the tools to challenge oppression.
- Intellectualism is the antidote to ignorance, the weapon of the enlightened.
- Intellectualism is the armour that shields us from the chains of oppression.
- Intellectualism is the bridge that connects us to the realm of possibilities.
- Intellectualism is the cornerstone of progress, shaping the destiny of nations.
- Intellectualism is the driving force behind innovation and revolution.
- Intellectualism is the flame that burns within, propelling us toward the light of freedom.
- Intellectualism is the foundation of critical thinking, empowering us to challenge the status quo.

- Intellectualism is the foundation of critical thinking, paving the way for positive change.
- Intellectualism is the key to unlocking the shackles of ignorance.
- Intellectualism is the light that illuminates the path to progress.
- Intellectualism is the weapon of the enlightened, empowering us to fight for freedom.
- It is a self-deception that attains India's political liberty through peaceful and legitimate means.
- It is all very well to hold fast to the highest ideal worthy of a nation, but it is necessary to adopt the best, the most productive and tried means to achieve it, or you become the laughing stock of the whole world.
- It is beyond the power of any man to make a revolution. Neither can it be brought about on any appointed date. Unique environments, social and economic, bring it about. The function of an organized party is to utilize any such opportunity offered by these circumstances.
- It is easy to kill individuals, but you cannot kill ideas. Great empires crumbled while the ideas survived.

- It is wrong to assign the widespread awakening of the masses to non-violence, which manifests wherever a direct-action program is adopted.
- It takes courage to dream but bravery to pursue those dreams against all odds.
- It was essential to warn timely that the people's unrest was increasing and that the sickness may take a serious turn if not treated adequately.

❑

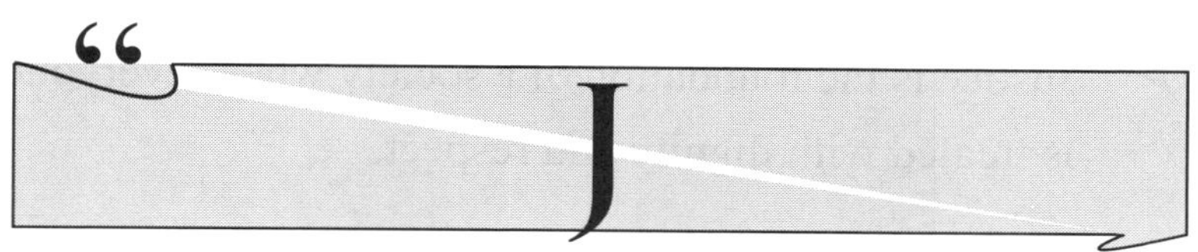

- Jails should be reformatories and not veritable hells.
- Justice is not a privilege but a fundamental human right.
- Justice is not just an ideal but a duty we owe to humanity.
- Justice is the beacon that leads us toward a better and fairer world.
- Justice is the cornerstone of a progressive and harmonious society.
- Justice is the essence of humanity, and it is our responsibility to uphold it.
- Justice is the foundation of a genuinely free and equitable society.

- Justice is the foundation of a society where all get treated with dignity and respect. In the face of oppression, resistance is the courage to stand up and speak out against tyranny.
- Justice is the foundation of a society where everyone is treated with dignity and respect.
- Justice is the light that dispels the darkness of oppression.
- Justice is the pillar on which a just and inclusive society stands.
- Justice is the sword that cuts through the chains of oppression.
- Justice is the voice of the oppressed, and we must amplify it.

❑

- Knowledge is power, and intellectualism is the key to unlocking that power.

❑

- Labour is the real sustainer of society.
- Leadership is about being accountable and responsible for one's actions and decisions.
- Leadership is about being courageous and taking bold decisions for the greater good.
- Leadership is about empowering others to become leaders in their right.
- Leadership is about fostering a sense of unity and inclusivity among people.
- Leadership is about leading with integrity, honesty, and humility.
- Leadership is about setting an example and being a role model for others.

- Leadership is about standing up for what is right, even when circumstances are not favourable.
- Leadership is about the courage to challenge the status quo and bring about positive change.
- Leadership is not about being in the limelight but working toward a common goal.
- Leadership is not about being perfect but about learning, growing, and inspiring others.
- Leadership is not about commanding but about collaborating and listening to diverse perspectives.
- Leadership is not about dominating but about empowering and uplifting others.
- Leadership is not about holding power but about empowering others.
- Leave sentimentalism aside. Be prepared to face the facts.
- Legacy is about being remembered for your positive impact on the world.
- Legacy is about creating a ripple effect of positive change that transcends time.

- Legacy is about making a difference, leaving the world a better place than you found it.
- Legacy is not about accumulating wealth or possessions but about leaving behind a legacy of values and principles.
- Legacy is not about what you leave behind but what you stand for.
- Let inspiration be your compass, guiding you toward your highest potential.
- Let inspiration be your driving force, and success will follow.
- Let intellectualism be your compass, guiding you toward truth and justice.
- Let justice be the guiding principle of your actions, for it is the cornerstone of righteousness.
- Let justice be the guiding star that leads us toward a better tomorrow.
- Let justice be the legacy we leave behind for future generations.
- Let nobody toy with the nation's freedom which is her very life, by doing psychological experiments in non-violence and other novelties.

- Let the fire of curiosity burn bright, driving you toward intellectual enlightenment.
- Let the fire of knowledge fuel your passion for freedom.
- Let the scales of justice always tip in favour of truth and fairness.
- Let the winds of inspiration carry you toward your destiny.
- Let the world know that India still thrives, that the blood of youth is still fired up, and that they can still risk their lives if their nation's honour is at stake.
- Let us declare that ordinances cannot cow our spirits once and for all.
- Let us establish a new order of society in which political and economic exploitation will be impossible.
- Let your activism shine like a beacon of hope, inspiring others to join the cause.
- Let your intellect be your guiding star, leading you towards a brighter future.
- Liberty is about breaking free from physical chains and the shackles of ignorance and injustice.

- Liberty is not a privilege bestowed by others but a right that belongs to all humanity.
- Liberty is the beacon of hope that shines in the darkest times, inspiring us to strive for a better tomorrow.
- Liberty is the birthright of every human being, and it is worth fighting for.
- Liberty is the essence of humanity and the driving force behind the pursuit of justice.
- Liberty is the foundation upon which the pillars of democracy stand, and it is a cause worth fighting for until the end.
- Liberty is the soul of a nation and the foundation upon which democracy is built.
- Life is a precious thing. It is dear to everyone.
- Life is all about learning.
- Love always elevates the character of the man. It never lowers him, provided love is love.
- Lovers, Lunatics, and poets are made up of the same stuff.

❑

- Man must try and endeavour because success depends on chance and the environment.
- Man must try hard to stick to his beliefs. No one can say what the future has in store.
- Martyrdom is a call to action, urging us to continue the struggle for justice, no matter the odds.
- Martyrdom is a legacy that lives on in the hearts of those who continue to carry the torch of freedom.
- Martyrdom is a reminder that freedom is not free and requires the utmost courage and sacrifice.
- Martyrdom is a testament to the unbreakable spirit of those willing to lay their lives for their beliefs.
- Martyrdom is not a defeat but a victory in the fight against injustice, tyranny, and oppression.

- Martyrdom is not a moment of defeat but a legacy of resilience and determination that lives on forever.
- Martyrdom is not the end but a beginning of a legacy that lives on forever.
- Martyrdom is not the end but a beginning of a new chapter in the quest for a just and equitable society.
- Martyrdom is the epitome of bravery and self-sacrifice, an example that shines through the annals of history.
- Martyrdom is the fuel that keeps the fire of revolution burning, inspiring us to continue the fight for justice.
- Martyrdom is the ultimate expression of love for one's country, a sacrifice that transcends time and space.
- Martyrdom is the ultimate testament to one's unwavering commitment to the cause of freedom and justice.
- May the sun in his course visit no land freer, happier, more lovely than this our country.
- Men must try and endeavour; success depends upon chance and environment.

- Merciless criticism and independent thinking are the two necessary traits of revolutionary thinking.
- Mere faith or blind faith is dangerous: it dulls the brain and makes a man reactionary.
- Misrepresentation is and has always been the best instrument in the hands of the Govt. to meet their enemies.
- Mixing arsenic (poison) in the flour will not be considered a crime, provided its purpose is to kill rats. But if the aim is to kill a man, it becomes a crime of murder.
- Motivation is the catalyst for change, propelling us to take action and make a difference.
- Motivation is the driving force that enables us to persevere in the face of adversity.
- Motivation is the driving force that propels us toward our vision of a better world.
- Motivation is the fire within us that fuels our passion for justice and freedom.
- Motivation is the force that empowers us to rise above challenges and strive for greatness.

- Motivation is the force that empowers us to stand up for justice, irrespective of the obstacles.
- Motivation is the foundation upon which revolutions are built, driving us to challenge the status quo.
- Motivation is the fuel that drives us to take action and strive for our ideals.
- Motivation is the inner drive that propels us to fight for our rights and the rights of others.
- Motivation is the inner fire that burns within us, urging us to never give up on our dreams.
- Motivation is the key that unlocks the door to success, empowering us to chase our dreams.
- Motivation is the spark that ignites the fire of revolution, propelling us toward our goals.
- My heart nurtured some ambitions to do something for humanity and my country.
- My life is dedicated to the noblest cause, the country's freedom. Therefore, no rest or worldly desire can lure me now.
- My life is not as precious, at least to me, as you may think.

❑

N

- Neither to become a king, nor to gain any other rewards here, or in the next birth or after death in paradise, shall they be inspired to challenge the oppressors, exploiters, and tyrants, but to cast off the yoke of serfdom from the neck of humanity and to establish liberty and peace shall they tread this—to their selves perilous and to their noble selves the only glorious imaginable-path.
- Never for a moment did I desire to save my neck at the cost of certain other things.
- Never regards undertrial prisoners as convicted prisoners.
- Never underestimate the power of change, for it has the potential to transform the world and shape the course of history.

- No difficulties and no hardships shall discourage you.
- No failure and betrayal shall dishearten you.
- No man can claim to know a people's mind by seeing them from the public platform and giving them 'Darshan' and 'Updesh.'
- No more mysticism, no more blind faith! Realism became our cult.
- No obstacle is insurmountable with perseverance as our guide, which fuels our determination to achieve the impossible.
- No one can do justice to anybody without considering his motive.
- No one can ever extinguish the desire for liberty inherent in every human heart.
- No one can find the motive behind the offence of an accused without knowing his psychology.
- None whose heart bleeds for them, who have given their life-blood in silence to the building up of the economic structure, could repress the cry that this cruel blow had wrung out of our hearts.

- Non-violence is backed by the theory of soul force, in which suffering is ultimately courted to win over the opponent. But what happens when such an attempt fails to achieve the object? Here, soul force must be combined with physical strength so as not to remain at the mercy of a tyrannical and ruthless enemy.

- Non-violence may be a noble ideal, but it is a thing of the morrow.

❑

- Official terrorism is sure to be met by counter-terrorism.
- Old order should constantly change, yielding place to new so that one good order may not corrupt the world. In this sense, we raise that shout 'Long Live Revolution.'
- One can shed a martyr's blood, but their ideals and principles continue to guide us in our pursuit of freedom.
- One friend asked me to pray. When informed of my atheism, he said, "During your last days, you will begin to believe." I said, "No, dear Sir, it shall not be. I will think that to be an act of degradation and demoralization. For selfish motives, I am not going

to pray. Readers and friends, Is this vanity? If it is, I stand for it."

- One of my revolutionary friends used to say that philosophy is the outcome of human weakness.
- Only counter-terrorism on the part of revolutionaries can checkmate this bureaucratic bullying effectively.
- Our line of thinking and that of a learned judge may differ, but that does not mean we are deprived of permission to express our ideas and that wrong things are to be propagated in our name.
- Our practical protest was against the institution, which has eminently helped display not only its worthlessness but its far-reaching power for mischief since its birth.
- Our real battle is against our disabilities, which the enemy and some of our people exploit for their selfish motives.
- Our slavery is our shame.

❑

- Passion is the catalyst for action, propelling us to take a stand and make a mark in history.
- Passion is the driving energy that propels us to challenge the status quo and strive for a better world.
- Passion is the driving force that empowers us to impact the world around us positively.
- Passion is the driving force that empowers us to pursue our dreams with unwavering determination.
- Passion is the driving force that empowers us to rise above challenges and pursue our vision.
- Passion is the driving force that empowers us to speak up, act boldly, and make a difference.
- Passion is the driving force that empowers us to stand up for justice, no matter the cost.

- Passion is the fire that burns within us, driving us to fight for our beliefs and the freedom of others.
- Passion is the fire that burns within us, urging us to never give up on our ideals.
- Passion is the fire that fuels our commitment to a cause, propelling us to persevere in the face of adversity.
- Passion is the fuel that ignites the fire of revolution, driving us toward our mission.
- Passion is the inner fire that drives us to strive for greatness and leave a legacy of impact.
- Passion is the spark that sets our hearts ablaze, propelling us to take action and make a difference.
- Patriotism is about waving flags and standing up for the values and principles that define our nation.
- Patriotism is not just a feeling; it's a commitment to serve and protect the ideals of our nation.
- Patriotism is the beacon that guides us toward a future where our nation shines with prosperity and inclusivity.
- Patriotism is the commitment to leave behind a legacy of progress and prosperity for our nation.

- Patriotism is the driving force that propels us to be active participants in shaping the destiny of our nation.
- Patriotism is the driving force that propels us to work tirelessly toward the progress and prosperity of our nation.
- Patriotism is the flame that burns within us, inspiring us to work toward the betterment of our nation.
- Patriotism is the force that compels us to work towards building a nation where every citizen gets treated with dignity and respect.
- Patriotism is the love for one's country that fuels the fire of revolution.
- Patriotism is the unbreakable bond that connects us to our nation's rich history, culture, and heritage.
- Patriotism is the unwavering belief in the greatness of one's country and the determination to make it even better.
- Patriotism is the unwavering belief that the freedom and well-being of our nation are worth every sacrifice.
- Peace and tranquillity you cannot achieve by peaceful and legitimate means.

- People holding ideas like ours do not throw bombs on their innocent people.
- People recognise the merits of socialism as much as the general welfare is concerned.
- Perseverance is the attitude that turns obstacles into opportunities and failures into stepping stones.
- Perseverance is the bridge that connects our dreams to reality, no matter how long the journey may be.
- Perseverance is the fire that burns within us, driving us to keep pushing forward, no matter how tough the battle.
- Perseverance is the fuel that keeps our dreams alive, no matter how many obstacles we encounter.
- Perseverance is the inner strength that keeps us going, even when our outer circumstances are challenging.
- Perseverance is the key that unlocks the door to success, no matter how challenging the path may be.
- Perseverance is the mindset that never settles but keeps striving for progress, growth, and success.
- Perseverance is the mindset that never settles for mediocrity but constantly strives for excellence.

- Perseverance is the quality that turns ordinary individuals into extraordinary achievers.
- Perseverance is the spirit that refuses to succumb to defeat but rises with renewed strength and determination.
- Perseverance is the unwavering commitment to our goals, despite the obstacles that may come our way.
- Perseverance is the unwavering determination to keep moving forward, even when things get tough.
- Perseverance is unwavering faith in oneself, even when the world doubts.
- Philosophy is the outcome of human weakness or limitation of knowledge.
- Poverty is a sin; it is a punishment.
- Pursuing justice requires us to stand up against injustice, no matter the cost.
- Pursuing knowledge is a lifelong journey that empowers us to break free from limitations.

❑

- Realism became our cult.
- Rebellion against the king is always a sin according to every religion.
- Rebellion expresses the indomitable human spirit, refusing to bow to injustice.
- Rebellion is breaking free from the chains of conformity, daring to challenge the norms, and envisioning a brighter future.
- Rebellion is the fire that burns within us, urging us to stand up for what is right and just.
- Rebellion is the force that shatters the chains of oppression, unleashing the power of freedom.
- Rebellion is the fuel that drives the wheels of revolution, paving the way for a brighter, more just future.

- Rebellion is the path chosen by those who refuse to accept oppression and fight for their rights with unwavering determination.
- Rebellion is the path of courageous people who refuse to accept injustice and take action to bring about change.
- Rebellion is the refusal to accept injustice, the determination to fight for what is right, no matter the consequences.
- Rebellion is the refusal to accept the status quo, the drive to create a better world for ourselves and future generations.
- Rebellion is the soul of freedom, the driving force that breaks the shackles of oppression and paves the way for liberation.
- Rebellion is the soul of revolution, empowering individuals to rise and fight against oppression.
- Rebellion is the spark that ignites the fire of change, challenging the status quo and paving the way for progress.
- Rebellion is the spirit that refuses to bow down, challenges unjust norms and fights for equality and liberty.

- Rebellion is the voice of the oppressed, the downtrodden, and the marginalized, demanding justice and freedom.
- Rebellion is the voice of the unheard, the strength of the weak, and the hope of the oppressed.
- Rebellion manifests our inherent human rights, asserting our dignity and freedom.
- Reformative theory is the only one essential and indispensable for human progress. It aims at returning the offender as a most competent and peace-loving citizen to society.
- Religion is the outcome of human weakness or the limitation of human knowledge.
- Resilience is an indomitable spirit within us that refuses to accept defeat and keeps pushing forward with unwavering determination.
- Resilience is the armour that protects us from the arrows of failure, disappointment, and setbacks.
- Resilience is the attitude that turns challenges into opportunities and setbacks into stepping stones.
- Resilience is the fire that burns within us, empowering us to overcome all obstacles and achieve our goals.

- Resilience is the foundation of strength, the ability to stand tall in the face of challenges and emerge victorious.
- Resilience is the fuel that keeps us going, even when the odds are stacked against us and the journey is tough.
- Resilience is the inner strength that keeps us going, even when the world tries to bring us down.
- Resilience is the power within us, enabling us to rise again, no matter how many times we fall.
- Resilience is the quality that separates the ordinary from the extraordinary. It is the ability to keep moving forward when others give up.
- Resilience is the strength that arises from adversity, the ability to bounce back in the face of challenges.
- Resilience is the tenacity that keeps us moving forward, even when the road is tough, and the challenges seem insurmountable.
- Resilience is the unwavering belief in oneself and the confidence to face adversity with courage and determination.
- Resistance is the call to action, the voice of the oppressed, and the path to freedom and equality.

- Resistance is the courage to challenge the system and the determination to create a more just and equitable society.
- Resistance is the force that empowers us to break free from the chains of oppression and create a better future.
- Resistance is the legacy of the brave, the spirit that lives on in the hearts of those who fight for freedom.
- Resistance is the refusal to accept the unacceptable and the relentless pursuit of equality and freedom.
- Resistance is the refusal to be silenced, the power to speak up and raise our voices against oppression.
- Resistance is the refusal to bow to injustice, the unwavering stand for what is right.
- Resistance is the strength that arises from the collective will of the people, united in the fight against oppression.
- Resistance is the strength that comes from standing up for our rights and fighting for what we believe in.
- Resistance is the unwavering belief in the power of change and the refusal to submit to injustice.
- Resistance is the unwavering faith in the power of change and the firm commitment to make it happen.

- Resistance is the weapon of the determined, the tool of the courageous, and the shield of the oppressed.
- Resistance is the weapon of the oppressed, the voice of the marginalized, and the power of the people.
- Revolution does not merely mean an upheaval or sanguinary strife. Revolution necessarily implies the systematic reconstruction of society on a new and better-adapted basis after the destruction of the existing state of affairs.
- Revolution does not necessarily involve sanguinary strife, nor is there any place for individual vendetta. It is not the cult of the bomb and the pistol.
- Revolution embodies courage, the audacity to challenge the existing norms and create a new reality.
- Revolution embodies the people's power, the force that shatters the chains of oppression and ushers in change.
- Revolution is a challenging task. It is beyond the power of any man to make a revolution.
- Revolution is a phenomenon that nature loves, without which there can be no progress in nature or human affairs.

- Revolution is a vital living force that indicates an eternal conflict between the old and the new, between life and living death, and between light and darkness.
- Revolution is an inalienable right of humankind. Freedom is an imperishable birthright of all. Labour is the real sustainer of society, the sovereignty of the ultimate destiny of the workers.
- Revolution is certainly not an unthinking, brutal campaign of murder and incendiarism; it is not a few bombs here and a few shots fired there; neither is it a movement to destroy all remnants of civilisation and blow to pieces time-honoured principles of justice and equity.
- Revolution is law; revolution is order; and revolution is the ultimate truth.
- Revolution is not just a moment in time but a movement that changes the course of history.
- Revolution is the catalyst for societal transformation, sparking the flame of change.
- Revolution is the collective awakening of the masses, realising their power, and the determination to break free from oppression.

- Revolution is the force that challenges the status quo, disrupts the existing order, and creates space for a new world to emerge.
- Revolution is the force that empowers the downtrodden, the marginalised, and the oppressed to rise and demand their rights.
- Revolution is the legacy of the brave, the path that has been trodden by those who dared to dream of a better world.
- Revolution is the spirit that lives on, carried forward by the legacy of those who fought for justice and equality.
- Revolution is the unwavering belief in the power of change and the relentless pursuit of equality and liberty.
- Revolution is the unwavering belief in the power of people and the determination to bring about social and political change.
- Revolution is the voice of the oppressed, the power of the people, and the hope for a better future.
- Revolution may be anti-God, but it is undoubtedly not anti-Man.

- Revolution was the vital living force indicative of eternal conflict between life and death, the old and the new, light and the darkness.
- Revolutionaries are the architects of societal change, envisioning a future where freedom, equality, and justice prevail.
- Revolutionaries are the beacons of hope, the guiding lights that inspire others to join the liberation struggle.
- Revolutionaries are the change-makers who refuse to accept the status quo and work tirelessly to transform the world.
- Revolutionaries are the dreamers who dare to imagine a world where everyone is treated with dignity and respect.
- Revolutionaries are the embodiment of sacrifice, willing to give up their comforts and even their lives for the cause.
- Revolutionaries are the trailblazers who challenge the existing norms and pave the way for a new order.
- Revolutionaries are the vanguard of change, the pioneers who dare to challenge the status quo.
- Revolutionaries are the warriors who fight for the rights and freedoms of their fellow citizens, undeterred by challenges.

- Revolutionaries are visionaries who see beyond the present and strive to create a better future for all.
- Revolutionaries are warriors who fearlessly confront tyranny and oppression to pursue freedom.
- Revolutionaries catalyse social transformation, sparking the flame of change and inspiring others to join the revolution.
- Revolutionaries embody resilience, overcoming challenges and obstacles with unwavering resolve.
- Rise above apathy and mediocrity, and embrace the power of activism.

❑

- Sacrifice embodies courage and bravery, requiring immense strength to give up comfort for the greater good.
- Sacrifice is not a burden, but a privilege, as it allows us to make a meaningful impact in the lives of others.
- Sacrifice is not a loss, but a gain, as it serves as an inspiration for others to continue the fight for liberation.
- Sacrifice is the bridge between dreams and reality, as it requires taking bold actions to bring about meaningful change.
- Sacrifice is the driving force that empowers ordinary individuals to become extraordinary revolutionaries.
- Sacrifice is the embodiment of courage, as it requires facing adversity with unwavering resolve and unwavering determination.

- Sacrifice is the essence of authentic leadership, as it requires putting the welfare of others above one's own.
- Sacrifice is the essence of revolution, as it requires individuals to put the cause above their interests.
- Sacrifice is the hallmark of those who are willing to give up everything for the cause of freedom and justice.
- Sacrifice is the price one pays for a higher purpose, a testament to the unwavering commitment to the cause of freedom.
- Sacrifice is the ultimate act of selflessness, a virtue that shines brightly in the hearts of genuine revolutionaries.
- Sacrifice is the ultimate expression of patriotism, a selfless act that elevates the spirit and ignites the flame of revolution.
- Satyagraha is insistent upon truth.
- Seek justice not just for yourself but for all those who are voiceless.
- Selflessness embodies love for humanity, a quality that transcends personal interests and works toward the betterment of all.

- Selflessness is not a weakness, but a strength, as it requires immense courage and compassion to put others first.
- Selflessness is the epitome of generosity, as it involves giving without expecting anything in return for the greater good.
- Selflessness is the essence of humanity, a virtue that connects us all and brings out the best in us.
- Selflessness is the essence of sacrifice, a virtue that fuels the fire of revolution and leads to meaningful change.
- Selflessness is the foundation of genuine empathy, as it allows us to understand and care for the needs of others.
- Selflessness is the foundation of true heroism, a quality that shines bright in the hearts of revolutionaries.
- Selflessness is the highest form of humanity, elevating the spirit and inspiring others to follow suit.
- Selflessness is the key to unlocking the true potential of humanity, as it involves putting others before oneself and working for the common good.
- Selflessness is the moral compass that guides us toward acts of kindness, compassion, and empathy.

- Self-reliance is always liable to be interpreted as vanity.
- Self-reliance is always liable to be interpreted as vanity. It is sad and miserable, but there is no help.
- Shake off the dreams of personal comfort. Then start to work. So that when a man can be in great distress having been betrayed and deserted by all friends, he may find consolation in the idea that an ever-true friend was still there to help him, to support him and that He was Almighty and could do anything. The concept of God is helpful to man in distress.
- Socialism calls for a just distribution of resources with equal access to opportunities and benefits.
- Socialism calls for social and economic equality, where the gap between the rich and the poor get narrowed, and opportunities are available to all.
- Socialism calls for solidarity and brotherhood, where the interests of the working class and the marginalized are protected and uplifted.
- Socialism is pursuing economic and social justice, where all, not just a privileged few, share the fruits of progress.

- Socialism is the antidote to poverty, inequality, and exploitation and the path toward a more equitable and inclusive world.
- Socialism is the belief in the collective welfare of society, where the needs of the many outweigh the greed of the few.
- Socialism is the belief in the dignity of labour, where workers are not exploited but empowered, and their rights are protected.
- Socialism is the belief in the power of collective action, where people come together to create a better society for all.
- Socialism is the belief in the power of community and cooperation, where people work together for the common good.
- Socialism is the belief that society should be organized to promote the welfare of all, not just a select few.
- Socialism is the call for a society where the means of production are owned and controlled by the people, and the benefits are shared by all.
- Socialism is the dream of a society where exploitation, oppression, and discrimination replace cooperation, equality, and fraternity.

- Socialism is the ideology of empowerment, where every individual has the right to dignity, equality, and a life of dignity.
- Socialism is the ideology that champions the cause of the downtrodden, the marginalized, and the oppressed and seeks to uplift their lives.
- Socialism is the path towards a society where the basic needs of every individual meet, and no one is left behind.
- Socialism is the path towards a world where wealth is not concentrated in the hands of a few but shared by the many for the benefit of all.
- Socialism is the philosophy of compassion and empathy, where the needs of the vulnerable get prioritized over the greed of the powerful.
- Socialism is the pursuit of the common good over individual gain, where the welfare of society takes precedence over narrow interests.
- Socialism is the vision of a just society where all share wealth and opportunities, and no one is left behind.
- Socialism is the vision of a society where all individuals have the right to education, healthcare,

and dignified life, irrespective of their socio-economic status.

- Socialism is the vision of a world where exploitation and oppression get replaced by justice, equality, and fraternity among all human beings.
- Socialism is the voice of the working class, the peasants, and the labourers, demanding their rightful share in the fruits of progress.
- Society can maintain the sanctity of the law only so long as it expresses the will of the people.
- Society has to fight out this belief as well as the thought of idol worship and the narrow conception of religion. Similarly, when man tries to stand on his legs and become a realist, he shall have to throw the faith aside and face all the distress and trouble in which the circumstances may throw him.
- Solidarity bridges different communities, religions, and backgrounds to pursue justice and freedom.
- Solidarity is the backbone of social change, which unites diverse voices into a powerful chorus for justice.

- Solidarity is the belief in the inherent dignity and worth of every human being and the commitment to upholding their rights and dignity.
- Solidarity is the bond that unites people in the fight against injustice, discrimination, and oppression.
- Solidarity is the collective strength that empowers individuals to challenge injustice and fight for equality.
- Solidarity is the commitment to fight against injustice, even when it does not affect us directly, because we recognise the importance of standing up for others.
- Solidarity is the cornerstone of social movements, where people join hands to create positive societal change.
- Solidarity is the courage to stand up for what is right, even when it is difficult or unpopular, because we believe in the power of collective action.
- Solidarity is the force that breaks the chains of oppression and paves the way for a better future.
- Solidarity is the foundation of a just society, where people stand up for each other and work toward common goals.

- Solidarity is the fuel that drives social movements and ignites the flames of change.
- Solidarity is the moral compass that guides us toward empathy, compassion, and action for the betterment of society.
- Solidarity is the power of coming together, transcending differences, and standing up for what is right.
- Solidarity is the spirit of compassion, empathy, and support toward marginalised and oppressed people.
- Solidarity is the spirit of humanity, the recognition that we are all part of a larger whole and that our destinies are intertwined.
- Solidarity is the spirit of inclusivity, where no one is left behind, and everyone is valued and respected.
- Solidarity is the spirit of mutual aid, support, and compassion that enables individuals to overcome challenges and achieve collective goals.
- Solidarity is the thread that weaves the fabric of social justice, binding us in our quest for a more equitable world.

- Solidarity is the understanding that our liberation is intertwined and that we must work together to break the chains of oppression.
- Solidarity is the unity of purpose, the strength of collective action, and the foundation of social change.
- Solidarity is the unwavering support for all human rights and dignity, regardless of race, religion, caste, or gender.
- Solidarity is the voice of the voiceless, the support for the weak, and the defence of the oppressed.
- Solidarity recognises that we are all in this together and that our struggles are interconnected.
- Sovereignty embodies the people's will, the collective power that shapes the course of history.
- Sovereignty is a nation's heartbeat, its people's pulse, and the foundation of its existence.
- Sovereignty is the assertion of our inherent rights and the refusal to be oppressed or subjugated by others.
- Sovereignty is the belief in all human beings' inherent dignity and rights and the commitment to protect and uphold them.

- Sovereignty is the birthright of every human being, the autonomy to chart our course and shape our future.

- Sovereignty is the cornerstone of democracy, the principle that everyone has the right to participate in decision-making and governance.

- Sovereignty is the driving force that fuels the struggle for independence, the conviction that a nation has the right to govern itself.

- Sovereignty is the essence of independence, the right to self-determination, and self-governance.

- Sovereignty is the flame of freedom that burns in the hearts of those who refuse to be enslaved and strive for liberation.

- Sovereignty is the foundation of freedom, the power to determine our path and choices.

- Sovereignty is the foundation of national pride, the belief that our nation has the right to determine its course and destiny.

- Sovereignty is the freedom to express ourselves, voice our opinions, and stand up for our beliefs.

- Sovereignty is the fuel that ignites the fire of revolution, the driving force that inspires people to rise against oppression and fight for their rights.
- Sovereignty is the inherent right of every individual and every nation to govern their destiny.
- Sovereignty is the legacy of our forefathers, the precious gift of freedom that we must cherish, protect, and pass on to future generations.
- Sovereignty is the power of the people, the force that empowers them to challenge injustice, tyranny, and oppression.
- Sovereignty is the principle of equality, the recognition that all individuals and nations have the same inherent rights and deserve to get treated with dignity and respect.
- Sovereignty is the realisation that we are the masters of our fate and have the power to shape a better future for ourselves and our nation.
- Sovereignty is the soul of a nation, the essence of its identity, and the guiding principle that shapes its aspirations and dreams.

- Sovereignty is the sovereignty of the people, the belief that ultimate power rests with the masses and not with a select few.

- Sovereignty is the spirit of self-reliance, the belief that we can manage our affairs and determine our destiny.

- Sovereignty is the spirit of self-respect, the recognition that we are not subjects but free individuals capable of shaping our destiny.

- Sow the seeds of disgust and hatred against British imperialism in the fertile minds of your fellow youth.

- Stand up, speak up, and rise with your activism to make a difference.

- Strength embodies resilience, courage, determination, and the driving force that propels you toward your goals.

- Strength is not just physical; it is the mental fortitude to withstand challenges and fight for what is right.

- Strength is physical prowess and mental and emotional resilience to overcome obstacles and keep moving forward.

- Strength is the ability to rise above limitations, push past boundaries, and achieve greatness.
- Strength is the ability to stay true to your principles, despite opposition and adversity.
- Strength is the ability to transform adversity into opportunity and to use challenges as stepping stones toward success.
- Strength is the belief in yourself and your abilities and the confidence to face any challenge head-on.
- Strength is the cornerstone of progress, the catalyst for growth, and the foundation of success.
- Strength is the courage to speak up against injustice, even when faced with adversity.
- Strength is the determination to fight for justice, equality, and freedom, regardless of the consequences.
- Strength is the force that empowers you to challenge the status quo and question oppressive systems.
- Strength is the fuel that powers the engine of change and the driving force behind revolutions.
- Strength is the inner fire that burns within, driving you to strive for excellence and make a difference.

- Strength is the inner power that rises in adversity and the belief in your capabilities to overcome challenges.
- Strength is the legacy of our ancestors, the gift of resilience that we carry within us, and the force that propels us toward a better future.
- Strength is the power to break free from oppression and fight for freedom.
- Strength is the power to break through limitations and to strive for excellence in everything you do.
- Strength is the power to inspire others, led by example, and create positive change in the world.
- Strength is the refusal to get silent and the courage to raise your voice for the voiceless.
- Strength is the resilience to bounce back from failures and to learn from setbacks.
- Strength is the resilience to keep going even when the going gets tough and to never give up on your goals.
- Strength is the unwavering commitment to your mission and the perseverance to keep going, no matter how difficult the path is.

- Strength is the unwavering determination to stand up for your beliefs, regardless of obstacles.
- Strength is the unwavering faith in your convictions and the determination to stand up for what you believe in, no matter the odds.
- Strength is the willingness to sacrifice for a higher cause and to put the needs of others above your own.
- Study so that you can meet the arguments of your opponents. Equip your ideology with supporting ideas. If you oppose a prevailing belief and criticize a great person (considered an incarnation), you will find that people will call you vain and egoist. The reason for this is mental ignorance. Logic and free thinking are the twin qualities that a revolutionary must inevitably possess. Say that Mahatmas, who are great, should not be criticized because they are above criticism, and for this reason, whatever they say about politics, religion, economics, and ethics is correct, and that whatever they say will have to be accepted, whether you believe it or not, reveals a mentality which cannot lead us to progress and is regressive.
- Success belongs to those who persevere through failures, setbacks, and hardships.

- Success comes to those who persevere and keep going even when the odds seem insurmountable.
- Success requires perseverance, which results from consistent effort, determination, and resilience.
- Success rewards those who persevere and never give up on their dreams, no matter how tough the journey.
- Suicide is a heinous crime. It is an act of complete cowardice.
- Swaraj is not only attained by the masses but also for the masses.

❑

- Terrorism instils fear in the hearts of the oppressors, brings hopes of revenge and redemption to the oppressed masses, it gives courage and self-confidence to the wavering, it shatters the spell of the superiority of the ruling class, and raises the status of the subject race in the eyes of the world because it is the most convincing proof of a nation's hunger for freedom.
- Terrorism is not a complete revolution, and the revolution is not complete without terrorism.
- That this world is 'Maya' or 'Mithya', a dream or a fiction, is apparent mysticism that has originated and developed by Hindu sages of old ages, such as Shankaracharya and others.

- The accurate measure of a legacy is the positive change it brings to society.
- The aim of life is no more to control the mind but to develop it harmoniously; not to achieve salvation here after, but to make the best use of it here below; and not to realise the truth, beauty, etc., suitable only in contemplation, but also in the experience of daily life; social progress depends not upon the ennoblement of the few but on the enrichment of democracy; we can achieve universal brotherhood only when there is an equality in opportunity – opportunity in the social, political and individual life.
- The best part of self-study for one is to suffer oneself.
- The best way to remove the prevailing dissatisfaction would be to classify the political prisoners into a separate class which may further get subdivided into two categories—one for those convicted of non-violent offences and the other for persons whose violations include violence.
- The bomb was necessary to awaken England from her dreams. We dropped the bomb on the floor of the assembly chamber to register our protest on behalf of those who had no other means left to express their

heart-rending agony. Our sole purpose was to make deaf people listen and share the heedless, timely warning. Others have as keenly felt as we have done, and from the seeming stillness of the sea of Indian humanity, a veritable storm is about to break out.

- The call for revolution is the call for transformation, the demand for justice, and the pursuit of freedom.
- The conservativeness and orthodoxy of the Hindus, extra-territorialism and fanaticism of the Mohammedans, and narrow-mindedness of the communities, in general, are always exploited by the foreign enemy.
- The course of the debate only confirmed our conviction that the labouring millions of India had nothing to expect from an institution that stood as a menacing monument to the strangling of the exploiters and the serfdom of the helpless labourers.
- The day shall usher in a new era of liberty when a large number of men and women, taking courage from the idea of serving humanity and liberating them from suffering and distress, decide that there is no alternative before them except devoting their lives to this cause. They will wage war against their

oppressors, tyrants, or exploiters, not to become kings, or to gain any reward here or in the next birth or after death in paradise, but to cast off the yoke of slavery, to establish liberty and peace they will tread this difficult, but glorious path.

- The day we find a significant number of men and women with the psychology who cannot devote themselves to anything other than the service of humankind and emancipation of the suffering humanity shall inaugurate the era of liberty.
- The dirty alliance between religious preachers and possessors of power brought the boon of prisons, gallows, knouts, and such theories for humankind.
- The doctrine of universal brotherhood demands the exploitation of man by man and nation by nation to be rendered impossible.
- The experience of a century-long and worldwide struggle between the masses and the governing class is their guide to their goal, and the methods they are following have never been to have failed.
- The fight for justice may be challenging, but it is worth fighting.

- The fight for justice may be long and arduous but worth undertaking.
- The fight for liberty may be arduous, but it is a battle that we all fought to secure the rights of all.
- The fight for liberty may be fraught with challenges, but it is a battle that is worth fighting until the end.
- The fire of freedom gets fuelled by inspiration, and it burns within.
- The fire of rebellion burns in the hearts of those who dream of a better world and take action to make it a reality.
- The flame of liberty can never get extinguished, for it gets fuelled by the indomitable spirit of those seeking justice.
- The flame of rebellion burns bright in the hearts of those who refuse to accept the chains of oppression and who strive for a better tomorrow.
- The food on which the tender plant of liberty thrives is the blood of the martyr.
- The foreigners have no right to rule over India, so they must be denounced and driven out.

- The fundamental causes of the failure of the effects of the Ghadar Party (1914-15) were ignorance, apathy, and sometimes active opposition of the masses.
- The future of India rests with the youth. They are the salt of the earth. Their promptness in suffering, daring courage, and radiant sacrifice prove that India's future in their hands is perfectly safe.
- The greater the number of such workers organized into a party, the great the chances of your success.
- The greatest sin in this world is to be poor.
- The idea of God is helpful to man in distress.
- The Indian people do not love their English masters; they do not want them to be here, but they do help the Britishers simply because they are afraid of them, and this very fear resists the Indians from extending their helping hands to the revolutionaries, not that they do not love them.
- The Indian revolutionaries are neither terrorists nor anarchists. They never aim to spread anarchy in the land, so they can never properly be called anarchists.
- The legacy of a freedom fighter will etch in the hearts and minds of those who carry the torch of freedom forward.

- The legacy of revolutionaries is a testament to their unwavering courage, determination, and sacrifice.
- The legacy of revolutionaries is the beacon of hope that shines through the darkness of oppression, guiding us toward liberation.
- The legacy of revolutionaries is the indelible mark they leave on history, inspiring generations to come.
- The legacy of sacrifice is the beacon of hope that guides us toward a better and more just society.
- The legacy of sacrifice is the enduring legacy of heroes whose selfless deeds inspire the coming generations.
- The legacy of sacrifice is the eternal flame that burns in the hearts of those willing to lay their lives for their beliefs.
- The legacy of selflessness is the eternal flame that lights the way toward a more compassionate, just, and inclusive society.
- The legacy of selflessness is the legacy of those who work selflessly for the welfare of others, leaving behind a legacy of love and service.
- The making of nations requires the self-sacrifice of thousands of obscure men and women who care

more for the freedom of their country than for their comfort or interest, their lives, or the lives of those they love.

- The man should think of himself as a rival of God, or he may begin to believe himself to be God.
- The more we have pondered, the more deeply we have been convinced that it exists only to demonstrate to the world India's humiliation and helplessness, and it symbolises the overriding domination of an irresponsible and autocratic rule.
- The most incredible legacy one can leave behind is the legacy of fighting for justice and freedom.
- The only forces to rely on to bring about any revolution, whether national or socialist, are the peasantry and the labour.
- The party should have iron discipline, and it need not necessarily be an underground party but rather the contrary.
- The party should start with the work of mass propaganda. It is essential.
- The path of bravery is not easy, but it is worth treading for the cause of freedom.

- The path to greatness gets paved with perseverance, determination, and unwavering resolve.

- The peasant who grows corn for all starves with his family; the weaver who supplies the world market with textile fabric has not had enough to cover his and his children's bodies; masons, smiths, and carpenters who raise magnificent palaces live like pariahs in the slums.

- The people will not be guided by our committing suicides to escape the difficulties; on the contrary, this will be quite a reactionary step.

- The political revolution does not mean the transfer of state (or more crudely, the power) from the hands of the British to the Indians, but to those Indians who are one with us to achieve the final goal, or to be more precise, to be transferred to the revolutionary party through popular support.

- The power of intellect is a force that can shape nations and change the world.

- The power of intellect knows no boundaries. It transcends all barriers.

- The power of rebellion lies in the courage to stand up against tyranny, oppression, and injustice.

- The power of resilience lies in the ability to rise above our circumstances and create a better future, no matter how challenging it may seem.
- The power of resistance lies in the ability to rise above fear and oppression and fight for a better tomorrow.
- The power of revolution lies in the collective action of the people, united in their pursuit of a just and equitable society.
- The prison does not contain and can never possess any magnetic power to attract people from outside. Nobody will commit offences only to come to jail.
- The pursuit of intellectualism is a journey that leads to self-discovery and empowerment.
- The pursuit of justice is a noble cause that requires unwavering determination.
- The pursuit of justice requires courage, conviction, and unwavering commitment.
- The pursuit of knowledge is a noble endeavour that leads to enlightenment.
- The pursuit of liberty requires sacrifice, but it is a sacrifice worth making for the sake of freedom.

- The quest for justice is a continuous battle that requires relentless effort.
- The quest for liberty is a journey that requires unwavering faith in the ideals of justice and equality.
- The quest for liberty may be challenging, but it is a journey necessary for the progress of society.
- The reforms get formed by the vigour, courage, self-sacrifice, and emotional conviction of the young men, who do not know enough to be afraid and feel much more than they think.
- The revolution will ring the death knell of capitalism and class distinctions and privileges.
- The revolutionaries believe that the deliverance of their country will come through revolution.
- The revolutionaries claim that their sacrifices have produced a tremendous change in the mentality of the people.
- The revolutionaries know better than anybody else that a socialist society can never get brought by violence but should grow and evolve from within.
- The revolutionaries must never forget that they are striving for a complete revolution.

- The revolutionaries never claim the reforms as their achievements. They raised the standard of independence long ago. They have lived for it.

- The revolutionary armies shall march to other lands not to rule or loot the people but to pull the parasitic rulers from their thrones and stop their blood-sucking exploitation.

- The revolutionary movement has unnerved the weak, has inspired the robust and healthy, and has confounded the worldly wise and the learned.

- The revolutionary party is not national but international because its ultimate object is to bring harmony to the world by respecting and guaranteeing the diverse interests of the different nations.

- The road to success is full of challenges, but we can navigate through any storm with perseverance as our compass.

- The romance of militancy dominated our predecessors. Now significant ideas ousted this way of thinking. No more mysticism! No more blind faith! Now realism was our mode of thinking. We can resort to extreme methods at times of terrible necessity, but violence produces opposite results in mass movements.

- The sooner we recognise that there can be no compromise between independence and slavery, the better.
- The sovereignty of the people is the ultimate destiny of the workers.
- The spirit force has to be combined with physical strength to not remain at the mercy of a tyrannical and ruthless enemy.
- The spirit of freedom gets ignited by inspiration, a flame that no one can extinguish.
- The spirit of liberty burns within the hearts of those willing to defy oppression and fight for their rights.
- The spirit of rebellion catalyses changes, driving us to question, challenge, and strive for a more just and equal society.
- The spirit of rebellion embodies courage, standing up against injustice, and fighting for what we believe in.
- The spirit of rebellion is the driving force behind revolutions, shaking the foundations of unjust systems.
- The spirit of rebellion is the fire that ignites the desire for change and the courage to challenge the status quo.

- The spirit of resilience is the beacon of hope that guides us through the storms of life towards a brighter tomorrow.
- The spirit of resilience is the driving force that keeps us going, even when the path is arduous, and the destination seems distant.
- The spirit of resilience is the fire that burns within us, propelling us to overcome obstacles and achieve greatness.
- The spirit of resilience is the light that shines through the darkest of times, guiding us towards a brighter future.
- The spirit of resistance is the beacon of hope that inspires us to stand up against injustice, no matter the consequences.
- The spirit of resistance is the driving force that fuels the revolution and brings about transformation.
- The spirit of resistance is the fire that burns within, driving us to fight for our rights and freedom.
- The spirit of resistance is the light that shines in the darkest of times, showing us the path to justice and equality.

- The spirit of resistance is the spark that ignites the flame of revolution and the driving force behind societal transformation.
- The spirit of revolution is a beacon of hope guiding us toward a future where everyone gets treated equally.
- The spirit of revolution is the driving force that fuels the fight for freedom and inspires us to challenge the existing norms.
- The spirit of revolution is the fire that burns within, driving us to challenge the status quo and fight for change.
- The spirit of revolution is the light that guides us through the darkness of oppression and leads us toward liberation.
- The spirit of revolution is the spark that ignites the passion for change and drives us to strive for a better tomorrow.
- The spirit of revolution should always permeate the soul of humanity so that the reactionary forces may not accumulate to check its eternal onward march.
- The spirit of revolutionaries embodies fearlessness as they stand up against all odds to bring about a better world.

- The spirit of revolutionaries inspires others to join the struggle and become agents of change.
- The spirit of revolutionaries is the driving force that propels the movement for change, fuelled by passion and purpose.
- The spirit of revolutionaries is the fire that burns within, driving them to fight for justice and freedom.
- The spirit of revolutionaries is the force that ignites the passion for change and propels the movement for freedom.
- The spirit of sacrifice is the driving force that propels us to go beyond our interests and work for the greater good.
- The spirit of sacrifice is the driving force that propels us to overcome fear and fight for what we believe in.
- The spirit of sacrifice is the epitome of love for one's country and fellow citizens, a driving force that surpasses personal desires.
- The spirit of sacrifice is the flame that burns within the hearts of those willing to pay any price for the cause of freedom.

- The spirit of sacrifice is the guiding light that shows us the path of righteousness and inspires us to make meaningful contributions to society.
- The spirit of selflessness is the driving force that propels us to work tirelessly for the upliftment of society and the betterment of all.
- The spirit of selflessness is the fuel that keeps the fire of revolution burning, as it requires us to work for the collective welfare of all.
- The spirit of selflessness is the guiding light that inspires us to put others before ourselves and work for the greater good.
- The spirit of selflessness is the light that shines in the darkest of times, inspiring us to keep going and make a positive impact.
- The spirit of selflessness is the true mark of a leader, as it requires leading by example and putting the welfare of others above one's own.
- The value of sacrifice is immeasurable, as it is the currency that purchases the freedom of future generations.
- The value of sacrifice is immeasurable, as it is the fuel that brightens the fire of revolution.

- The value of selflessness is immeasurable, as it is the cornerstone of social change and progress.
- The value of selflessness is immeasurable, as it is the driving force behind acts of kindness, generosity, and compassion.
- The wise man of India says it is absurd to cherish the hope that India will not get reconquered by force of arms. However, they forgot that a handful of Englishmen kept under subjugation by the power of guns, one-fifth of the human race.
- The world changes when individuals rise and demand changes, and we must be those change-makers.
- The world needs more activists than spectators. Be the change!
- The world needs more Bravehearts who dare to challenge the status quo and make a difference.
- The world of woes and miseries is a veritable, eternal combination of numberless tragedies. Not a single soul is delighted.
- The youth movement should organise study circles, class lectures, and the publication of leaflets,

pamphlets, books, and periodicals. It is the best recruiting and training ground for political workers.

- There is no alternative but to depend on yourself. Standing firm on your feet amid storms and strong winds is not child's play. In difficult times, vanity, if it remains, evaporates, and man cannot find the courage to defy beliefs held in common esteem by the people. If he revolts against such ideas, he has extraordinary strength. It is the exact situation now.
- There is no concord, no symphony, and no rhythm without revolution.
- They may kill me, but they cannot kill my ideas. They can crush my body, but they will not be able to destroy my spirit.
- Those revolutionaries who have luckily escaped the gallows should live and show the world that they can embrace the gallows for their ideals and bear the worst kind of torture in the dark, dingy prison cells.
- True bravery means never giving up, even when the road ahead seems unconquerable.
- True bravery means standing up for your beliefs, even when the odds are against you.

- True liberty is not granted but earned through the unwavering courage and determination to stand up for what is right.
- True liberty is not just the absence of chains but the presence of opportunities and possibilities for all.
- True patriotism lies in active activism for the welfare of the people.
- True patriots are not scared to challenge the injustices and inequalities existing within their country.

❑

- Use of force is justifiable when resorted to as a matter of terrible necessity. Non-violence is a policy indispensable for all mass movements.

❑

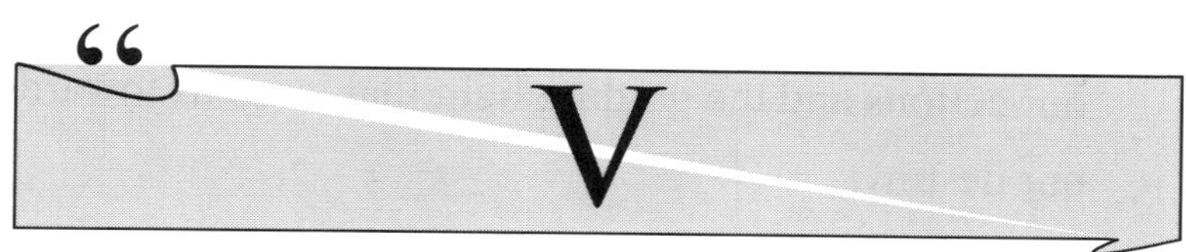

- Vanity or ‘Ahankar’ is the excess of undue pride in oneself.
- Violence is the physical force applied to commit injustice, and that is certainly not what the revolutionaries stand for.
- Vision is the ability to imagine the impossible, dream big, and take bold actions to transform those dreams into reality.
- Vision is the ability to see beyond the limitations of the present, envision a better world, and work tirelessly toward its realisation.
- Vision is the bridge between the present and the future, the guiding star that leads us toward our destiny, and the source of inspiration that propels us forward.

- Vision is the catalyst for change, the spark that ignites the flames of revolution, and the driving force behind social progress.
- Vision is the clarity of purpose that gives meaning to our actions and the guiding light that leads us toward our destiny.
- Vision is the clarity of purpose, the unwavering belief in a brighter future, and the determination to make that vision a reality.
- Vision is the courage to challenge the status quo, the audacity to dream of a better world, and the determination to make that dream a reality.
- Vision is the driving force that transforms dreams into reality, that turns aspirations into achievements, and propels us towards a brighter future.
- Vision is the force that empowers us to challenge the status quo, question the norms, and strive for a world where justice, equality, and freedom prevail.
- Vision is the foundation of leadership, the ability to inspire others with a compelling vision and rally them towards a common goal.

- Vision is the fuel that keeps us going when the going gets tough, the beacon of hope that shines in the darkest of times, and the North Star that guides us on our journey.
- Vision is the fuel that powers ambition, the inspiration that fuels innovation, and the catalyst for positive change.
- Vision is the gift of foresight, the ability to anticipate challenges and to prepare for the future with courage and conviction.
- Vision is the guiding light that illuminates our path, the driving force that propels us towards our goals, and the unwavering belief in our capabilities.
- Vision is the power to imagine a future better than the present and the determination to work towards that future with unwavering resolve.
- Vision is the power to see possibilities where others see limitations, envision a world without oppression, and strive toward that vision with unwavering resolve.
- Vision is the roadmap to success, the compass that guides us through challenges, and the beacon of hope amid darkness.

- Vision is the seed of change, the spark that ignites revolutions, and the driving force that propels humanity forward.
- Vision is the source of inspiration that fuels our passions, the compass that guides us on our journey, and the beacon of hope that keeps us going.

❑

- We are next to none in our love for humanity. Far from having any malice against any individual, we hold human life sacred beyond words.
- We become abject and ridiculous when we imbibe an unreasoned mysticism in life without any natural or substantial basis. People like us, who are proud to be revolutionary in every sense, should always be prepared to bear all the difficulties, anxieties, pains, and sufferings that we invite upon ourselves by the struggles initiated by us and for which we call ourselves revolutionary.
- We believe in nature. The whole progressive movement aims for the sovereignty of man over nature for his services.

- We believe in violence, not as an end but as a means to a noble end.
- We can break free from oppression with unwavering motivation and create a better future.
- We can create a world where justice and freedom thrive with passion as our guiding light.
- We can navigate through challenges and achieve our goals with motivation as our compass.
- We can never hope to win our freedom by mere non-violence.
- We can overcome any obstacle and achieve the impossible with passion as our guide.
- We despise hypocrisy.
- We do not believe in God, hell and heaven, punishment and rewards that are any Godly accounting of human life.
- We find nothing more important than the history and conditions of our country and its aspirations.
- We find vast differences in the fundamentals of various religious creeds, which sometimes assume extremely antagonistic and conflicting shapes.

- We hold human life sacred beyond words and would sooner lay down our lives in the service of humanity than injure anyone else.
- We must always maintain a clear goal for the achievement of freedom. It will help us determine the success and failures of our movements and enable us to formulate further plans quickly.
- We require—to use the term so dear to Lenin—the professional revolutionaries—the whole-time workers with no other ambitions or life-work except the revolution.
- We swear to die fighting but not to go to prison.
- We take this opportunity to appeal to our countrymen—the youth, the workers and peasants, the revolutionary intelligentsia—to come forward and join us in carrying the banner of freedom.
- We want people ready to fight without hope, fear and hesitation. We want people who are willing to die unhonoured, unwept and unsung.
- We want the economic liberty of the masses, and we are striving to win political power for that very purpose. No doubt, in the beginning, we shall have

to fight for little economic demands and privileges of these classes.

- We want to serve humanity as much as possible.
- We will sacrifice our all while serving our country.
- We wish for a world without unjust treatment, and people should not declare any biased opinion about us.
- We wished to get the maximum value for our lives.
- We would particularly emphasise that no political prisoner, whatever his offence, should be given any hard and undignified labour for which he may not feel the aptitude.
- We, the revolutionaries, are striving to capture power in our hands and to organise a revolutionary government that should employ all its resources for mass education.
- When a branch of a 'peepal' tree gets cut, then the religious feelings of the Hindus get injured.
- When a revolutionary believes certain things to be his right, he asks for them, plead for them, argues for them, wills to attain them with all the spirit

force at his command, stands significant amount of suffering for them, is always prepared to make the highest sacrifice for their attainment, and also backs his efforts with all the physical force he is capable of.

- When hope fades, let inspiration guide you towards the light.
- When man tries to stand on his legs and become a realist, he must throw faith aside and boldly face all the challenges and obstacles that circumstances may throw at him.
- When motivation takes hold, ordinary individuals can achieve extraordinary feats.
- When our ancestors had enough leisure time to try to solve the mystery of this world, its past, present, and future, its whys and wherefores, having been short of direct proofs, everybody tries to solve the problems in their way.
- When passion takes hold, ordinary individuals can achieve extraordinary feats.
- When the enemy is determined to break the peace at his convenience, the legitimate power loses all its

charm and significance when one pledges oneself to maintain peace at all costs.

- When the fate of a country is determined, people should forget about the future of the individuals.
- When the world says ‘give up’, perseverance whispers ‘try one more time’.
- Where direct proofs are lacking, faith occupies a significant place.
- Whether violent or non-violent, successful or unsuccessful, mass action is bound to produce the same kind of repercussion on the finances of a state.
- While the revolutionaries stand to achieve independence by all forces, physical or moral, at their command, the advocates of non-violence would like to ban the use of physical force.
- While we worked, we became targets of many kinds of difficulties.
- With all its prejudices and conservatism, human nature has an instinctive dread of revolution.
- With all the strength at my command, let me announce that I am not a terrorist, and I never was, except

perhaps at the beginning of my revolutionary career. And I am convinced that we cannot gain anything through those methods.

- With inspiration as our ally, we can conquer any mountain.
- With inspiration as our guide, we can achieve the impossible.
- With inspiration in our hearts, we can move mountains and create history.
- With motivation as our guide, we can overcome every obstacle and achieve greatness.
- With motivation as our guiding force, we can create a world of justice and freedom.
- With motivation as our guiding light, we can overcome fear and make our voices heard.
- With no selfish motive or desire to be awarded here or hereafter, quite disinterestedly have I devoted my life to the cause of independence because I could not do otherwise.
- With passion as our compass, we can navigate challenges and leave a mark of change.

- With passion as our driving force, we can overcome fear and make our voices heard.
- With unwavering motivation, we can break through the barriers of oppression and achieve freedom.
- With unwavering passion, we can break free from the chains of oppression and create a legacy of change.
- With unwavering passion, we can break through the barriers of oppression and create a world of justice.

❑

- You and I did not give birth to ideas of socialism and communism in the country; this is the consequence of the effects of our time and situations upon ourselves.
- You cannot expect a sailor to stop his ship and land every twenty-four hours to do his four hours of daily labour to earn his livelihood or a scientist to leave his laboratory and his experiment (work) to do his quota in the field. Both of them are doing very productive labour. The only difference the socialist society expects is that the mental workers shall no longer get regarded as superior to the manual workers.
- You may crush specific individuals, but you cannot destroy the nation.
- You will live, and while living, you will have to show the world that the revolutionaries die for their ideals and face every calamity.

- Young men and women have written human progress history with their blood.
- Young men who may have matured their ideas and are ready to devote their lives to the cause may get transferred to the party.
- Young men, awake, arise; we have slept too long!
- Youngsters are dreamers, believers, and doers with the power to turn their dreams into reality and impact society.
- Your legacy is not just measured by the number of years you live but by the impact you make in the lives of others.
- Your legacy is not what you accomplish but the inspiration you ignite in others.
- Your legacy is the impression you leave on the world, a beacon of hope for future generations.
- Your legacy is the imprint you leave on the world. It is the reflection of your values and beliefs.
- Your legacy is your contribution to the world, a testament to your purpose and passion.
- Your legacy is your story. It is up to you to make it a tale of inspiration and impact.

- Your silence won't change the world, but your activism will.
- Youth is not just a phase of life. It is a state of mind that can change the world.
- Youth is the fire that burns within; the passion that drives us forward; and the determination that keeps us going, irrespective of the challenges.
- Youth is the spirit of change, the energy that fuels revolutions, and the voice that demands a better world.
- Youth is the time for action, to take charge of our destiny, and to shape the world according to our vision.
- Youth is the time to challenge the status quo, question the norms, and strive for a world where freedom, equality, and justice prevail.
- Youth is the time to dream big, question the status quo, and challenge the norms for a better tomorrow.
- Youth is the time to rise above limitations, break free from the shackles of tradition, and create an inclusive and just future.

- Youth is the time to rise, stand up against oppression, and fight for the rights and dignity of all.
- Youth is the vanguard of change, the driving force that can bring about social, political, and economic transformation.
- Youth is the voice of change, the catalyst for progress, and the hope for a brighter future.
- Youths are not just a demographic but a powerful force that can bring positive change. Also, they are competent enough to challenge the existing order and bring about a revolution.
- Youths are not just our future, but they are also our present, with the power to make a difference and shape the destiny of a nation.
- Youths are the agent of transformation. They are the generation that can break free from the chains of conformity and create a new world.
- Youths are the beacon of hope that leads to a better future. They are the driving force that propels us towards a great future.
- Youths are the flame of rebellion that burns bright with the desire for freedom, justice, and equality.

- Youths are the force that challenges the status quo, pushes boundaries, and leads the way towards progress and social transformation.
- Youths are the powerhouse of energy, passion, and idealism. They are capable of beginning revolutions and transforming societies.
- Youths are the reservoir of ideas, dreams, and aspirations. They have the power to shape the destiny of a nation and inspire generations.
- Youths are the reservoir of talent, innovation, and creativity. They are capable of solving the most pressing challenges of society.
- Youths embody courage, resilience, and determination, with the potential to overcome any obstacle and achieve the impossible.